THE RENAISSANCE PRINCES

TREASURES OF THE WORLD

THE RENAISSANCE PRINCES

by

Olivier Bernier

STONEHENGE

Treasures of the World was created by
Tree Communications, Inc.
and published by Stonehenge Press Inc.

TREE COMMUNICATIONS, INC.

PRESIDENT
Rodney Friedman

PUBLISHER
Bruce Michel

VICE PRESIDENTS
Ronald Gross
Paul Levin

EDITOR
Charles L. Mee, Jr.

EXECUTIVE EDITOR
Shirley Tomkievicz

ART DIRECTOR
Sara Burris

PICTURE EDITOR
Mary Zuazua Jenkins

TEXT EDITOR
Henry Wiencek

ASSOCIATE EDITORS
Thomas Dickey   Vance Muse   Artelia Court

ASSISTANT ART DIRECTOR
Carole Muller

ASSISTANT PICTURE EDITORS
Deborah Bull   Carol Gaskin
Charlie Holland   Linda Silvestri Sykes

COPY EDITOR
Fredrica A. Harvey

ASSISTANT COPY EDITOR
Cynthia Villani

PRODUCTION MANAGER
Peter Sparber

EDITORIAL ASSISTANTS
Carol Epstein   Martha Tippin
Holly McLennan Wheelwright

FOREIGN RESEARCHERS
Rosemary Burgis (London) Bianca Spantigati Gabbrielli (Rome)
Patricia Hanna (Madrid) Alice Jugie (Paris)
Traudl Lessing (Vienna) Dee Pattee (Munich)
Brigitte Rückriegel (Bonn) Simonetta Toraldo (Rome)

CONSULTING EDITOR
Joseph J. Thorndike, Jr.

STONEHENGE PRESS INC.

PUBLISHER
John Canova

EDITOR
Ezra Bowen

DEPUTY EDITOR
Carolyn Tasker

ADMINISTRATIVE ASSISTANT
Elizabeth Noll

THE AUTHOR: Olivier Bernier, a translator and historian who lives in New York City, is the author of *Pleasure and Privilege* and *The Eighteenth Century Woman.* Currently he is at work on a full-length biography of Louis XV.

CONSULTANT FOR THIS BOOK: Colin Eisler, who specializes in the painting and graphic arts of the Renaissance, is Robert Lehman Professor of Fine Arts at the Institute of Fine Arts of New York University.

Published simultaneously in Canada.
Library of Congress catalogue card number 82-50158
ISBN 0-86706-083-2
ISBN 0-86706-084-0 (lib. bdg.)
ISBN 0-86706-085-9 (retail ed.)
STONEHENGE with its design is a registered trademark of Stonehenge Press Inc.
Printed in U.S.A. by R.R. Donnelley & Sons.
For reader information about any Stonehenge book, please write: Reader Information/ Stonehenge Press Inc./303 East Ohio Street/Chicago, Illinois 60611.

COVER: *Princely emblems—Florentine lilies adopted by the Medici—stand braced by the tails of fantastic dolphins in the center of an Italian table made of inlaid semiprecious stones.*

TITLE PAGE: *Handsome and gifted, Giuliano de' Medici, brother of Lorenzo the Magnificent, was the embodiment of Renaissance panache. Sandro Botticelli, a Medici favorite, idealized him in this portrait probably painted in 1478, the year Giuliano was brutally murdered in a political conspiracy.*

OVERLEAF: *Guests in gold brocade stroll under a striped awning at a fifteenth-century upper-class wedding. This scene adorns a painted frieze.*

ABOVE: *The left foot of the biblical hero David— sculpted by the Florentine Donatello—rests idly on the severed head of his enemy Goliath. This elegant, life-size bronze nude stood in the courtyard of the Medici palace at the wedding of Lorenzo.*

CONTENTS

VENICE

Venice

Padua

MANTUA

Mantua

FERRARA

Ferrara

MILAN

Milan

Novara

SAVOY

MONFERRATO

ASTI

SALUZZO

Piacenza   Busseto

Parma

Po

Fornovo di Taro

Borgotaro
(Borgo Val di Taro)

Modena

MODENA

Bologna

GENOA

Genoa

LUCCA

Prato

Florence

FLORENCE

Pisa

Arno

TUSCANY

Siena

Volterra

SIENA

LIGURIAN SEA

RENAISSANCE ITALY
1494

0   75 Mi

0   75 Kil

BORGIA   **FARNESE**   **MEDICI**

ESTE   **GONZAGA**   **SFORZA**

Castro

Late in the fifteenth century, Italy was a hodgepodge of contentious independent states. Six great families—represented by the symbols above—held sway over the cities where those symbols appear. The inset map, opposite, shows the European powers that played important roles in Italy at that time.

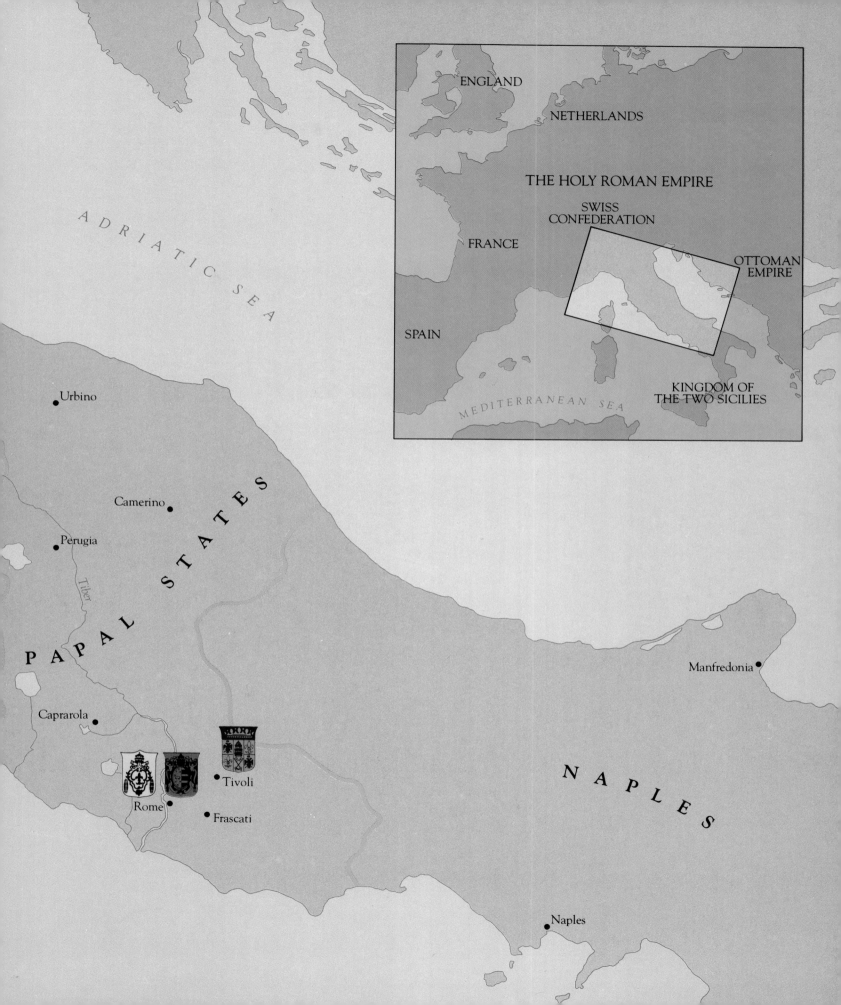

ADRIATIC SEA

THE HOLY ROMAN EMPIRE

ENGLAND

NETHERLANDS

SWISS
CONFEDERATION

FRANCE

OTTOMAN
EMPIRE

SPAIN

MEDITERRANEAN SEA

KINGDOM OF
THE TWO SICILIES

Urbino

P A P A L   S T A T E S

Camerino

Perugia

Tiber

Caprarola

Manfredonia

Rome

Tivoli

Frascati

N A P L E S

Naples

I

LORENZO THE MAGNIFICENT

AND THE EARLY MEDICI

Europe in 1469 numbered many ancient realms and countless noble families; but few kings were as rich or powerful as Piero de' Medici—an unassuming banker who, along with his friends, ran the government of Florence. And when Piero's son Lorenzo began to celebrate his betrothal in February 1469, the festivities were as splendid as anything the greatest monarch could devise.

Preceded by nine trumpeters, three pages, two squires, twelve nobles on horseback, and his younger brother Giuliano—who was wearing a brocade tabard, a doublet embroidered with pearls and silver, and jeweled feathers in his velvet cap—Lorenzo de' Medici himself arrived, a picture of splendor. Introduced by a corps of drummers and fifers, he rode into the Piazza Santa Croce—the square where jousts and games were held—on a magnificent horse caparisoned in red and white velvet embroidered with pearls. Lorenzo himself wore a fortune in gold thread, pearls, rubies, and diamonds. After a carefully organized tournament, the judges proclaimed Lorenzo the victor and awarded him a silver helmet that

Poet, philosopher, and ruler, Lorenzo de' Medici brought Florence to its zenith. The sculptor Andrea del Verrocchio made this terra-cotta bust before 1488.

bore the figure of Mars, the Roman god of war. But the celebration was only just beginning; the bride had yet even to leave Rome. After she arrived in Florence, the Medici staged a feast for eight hundred of the citizens of the city, a banquet of many courses for some two thousand guests, and rejoicings for another three days.

The center of this extravaganza, the twenty-year-old Lorenzo, was not inherently attractive, having an awkward, ill-proportioned figure and a remarkably ugly face with small eyes, a bilious complexion, and a curiously flattened nose. But never have appearances been so deceptive. Lorenzo was friendly, outgoing, and full of zest and energy. Under his father's thoughtful guidance, he had grown up in the museumlike atmosphere of the new Medici palace—a bold, innovative piece of architecture that broke with the traditional medieval style. Lorenzo's grandfather Cosimo, who died when Lorenzo was fifteen, had been the first Medici to rule Florence and, despite his extreme generosity to charities, had made a fortune for the family. But Cosimo's greatest contributions to the life of his family and of Florence touched the artistic and scholastic worlds; he patronized numerous artists, and he founded the Medici library as well as an academy for Greek studies.

Piero sought to continue Cosimo's example and make Lorenzo into a prototype of the new Renaissance man—someone who could draw on the cultures of ancient Greece and Rome, as well as that of medieval Italy; appreciate and write poetry; discuss philosophy with the greatest scholars; understand and finance the most talented artists; grasp politics and rule effectively, smoothly, even justly.

These were great expectations, but Florence provided the perfect setting for the making of such a Renaissance man. The city was in the midst of a dazzling cultural explosion during which interest in painting and architecture revived, scholars rediscovered the glories of Greece and Rome, sailors charted the world. Piero's library held more volumes than any other, and he opened it to all. His gardens were adorned with antique sculptures that provided inspiration for such great sculptors as the young Michelangelo.

The Medici family was both rich and intelligent. To choose

With its crenellated walls and feudal towers, Florence resembled a medieval city in the late fifteenth century, when over fifty thousand people lived there. Stone bridges spanned the Arno River, flowing through town from the distant hills. The new cathedral dome, at left above, dominated the skyline.

Lorenzo's fiancée, the Medici went outside the city for the first time in order to form an alliance, just as other ruling families did. Clarice Orsini, Lorenzo's bride, was the daughter of a great Roman noble family, whose power would now work to enhance Piero's: a remarkable achievement in a highly class-conscious world.

Politically, the world was in a state of flux. The Eastern Roman Empire, with its capital in Constantinople, had endured for over a thousand years. Now, after resisting a variety of enemies, the once-powerful empire, weakened by its own internal dissensions, found itself confronted by a fearless warrior-people, the Turks, who swept in from the steppes of Asia. In 1439 the emperor John Paleologus, accompanied by the patriarch of Constantinople, had attended a council in Florence in an attempt to reunite the Eastern and Western Churches so that the West would be more likely to help him.

His mission failed, for in 1453 Constantinople fell to the Turks. But Paleologus did succeed in an unintended mission. He had brought books and learned men with him to the council, and after the fall of Constantinople, scholars migrated en masse to Florence. They had a powerful influence on the Florentines. Greek had for years been a dead, undecipherable language. But now, for the first time since the onset of the Middle Ages, the Italians learned enough Greek to read the works of Plato and Aristotle—the chief philosophers of Athens—and they rediscovered the great Roman authors in copies that had not been disfigured by the centuries or by careless, ignorant copyists.

Young Lorenzo was immediately influenced, for not only did he study Italian literature and Latin, but he also developed a devouring interest in Neoplatonism—the new philosophy taught by his tutor, Marsilio Ficino. Combining the Platonic cult of ideas with mystical longings and Christian precepts, Neoplatonism provided the perfect philosophic blend for the times. It also provided the perfect rationale for the kind of oligarchic rule the Medici had already established. Ficino taught Lorenzo the importance of classical cultures along with the brilliance of the new Italian achievements.

The Florentines needed money for their pursuits, and two great

Florentine banks issued gold coins in such large quantities that the minted florins became an international medium of exchange. In the detail above, from the cover of an account book published in nearby Siena, an official pays city workers.

innovations had already provided the necessary wealth: banking and the use of credit. European trade in the fifteenth century consisted of two main commodities: spices and cloth—mostly wool, but also silk. Venice, with its maritime empire, supplied the spices; but Florence organized the trade routes across northern Europe to take wool from England to the Netherlands (today's Holland and Belgium), where it was spun and woven; then to France; and on to Italy. To facilitate these complex transactions—and to get around the need to send bags of gold from one end of Europe to another—the Italians invented the letter of credit. A merchant might sell his cloth in Florence but then collect the money in Gent, for example, from the local branch of the Medici bank. Since the Church prohibited the charging of interest, the bankers made their profit by taking a premium on the exchange from one currency to the other. By 1450 Florence had emerged as the major banking city in Europe and thus the richest. Consequently the Medici, the leading banking family in Florence, made staggering yearly profits.

The city also had it industries. It produced fine woolen cloth and silk of extraordinary quality. Florence's goldsmiths and jewelers ranked among the finest in Europe. As a result Florence (with Milan, Venice, Rome, and Naples) reigned as one of the five great Italian powers—the Big Five. The word "Italy," in fact, usually referred to no more than a geographic location. Politically the peninsula contained a variety of independent countries: city-states such as Florence, Genoa, or Venice; duchies such as Milan, Ferrara, or Urbino; one kingdom, Naples; and in and around Rome, the Papal States—governed directly by the pope. Wars were frequent, though generally bloodless since the armies primarily consisted of mercenaries who valued their own lives. The smaller states constantly struggled to avoid being swallowed up by the five major ones. Each of these, in turn, engaged in a balancing act with the others to prevent any one competitor from growing too large and powerful.

The relative positions of the Big Five were also modified by rivalries among the other European states. Spain, newly united under Ferdinand and Isabella, was fast becoming a major power with

Sicily and the kingdom of Naples under her sway. France, fully recovered at last from the Hundred Years' War, now had the largest population and one of the most abundant food supplies of any nation in Europe. Separated by the nearly impassable barrier of the Pyrenees, Spain and France had traditionally been on amicable terms. They grew hostile when the French invoked their claim to Naples. Two centuries earlier Naples' king had been a member of the French royal family, and now France wanted Naples for her own.

Spain, however, felt strongly about being a Mediterranean power and was determined to prevent France from reclaiming its lost kingdom. The situation would become especially tense toward the end of the fifteenth century. Ferdinand and Isabella's grandson, the future Emperor Charles V, would be in line to inherit not just Spain as Charles I, but—through a shrewd dynastic alliance—also the Netherlands and the Holy Roman Empire. France would then face a potentially hostile power at every border except the one with Italy. Charles VIII of France would want to right the balance, and Italy—divided into rival states—would clearly provide the place to do it. Any true Italian statesman needed, therefore, to address the danger of the impending invasion by preparing a united front.

If Italy was divided and unstable, so was Florence. Hereditary monarchs ruled most European countries, but Florence was an oligarchic republic: the rich citizens, in effect, controlled the government with a constitution so complex as to be unworkable. A variety of governing boards—none of which could rule without the others—made sure that no one man would ever take over. In fact by the mid-fifteenth century, the various governing boards were composed largely of Medici followers. Thus, while Piero's status was that of an ordinary citizen, everyone knew he acted—like Cosimo before him—as the effective head of state. Still, his situation was inherently unstable and required a good deal of finesse.

In this uncertain political atmosphere the Medici gathered a treasure trove of rare and beautiful objects: cups, boxes, pots of gold-mounted alabaster, onyx, and other semiprecious stones. Tapestries deep with colors covered their walls. The silks, brocades, and velvets

Cosimo de' Medici—Lorenzo's grandfather, called Cosimo the Elder—astride a dainty white horse, returns to Florence, in 1434, from a year in voluntary exile. In this sixteenth-century painting by the artist, architect, and art historian Giorgio Vasari, the Florentines are happy to have him back.

15

FAR FROM THE MADDING CROWD

As rich as life was for the city's leaders in Florence, they needed respite from its distractions, disease, and dangers. The Medici owned a number of palatial country villas surrounded by gardens, and, about 1450, Cosimo the Elder built yet another at Cafaggiolo—north of Florence in the Mugello Valley.

Cosimo hired the architect and sculptor Michelozzo di Bartolommeo to convert an old castle in the Medici ancestral village into what would become the villa where the family would spend both its happiest and its most frightening times. The great Michelozzo retained the medieval, defensive features of the original castle, and the towers, battlements, moat, and drawbridge at Cafaggiolo served the family well when they fled there after an attempted assassination of Lorenzo. While Cafaggiolo did provide refuge from enemies—and the family could rely on the villa's self-sufficient farm—it was chiefly a pleasure palace. Behind the well-protected walls of Cafaggiolo, the Medici played host to their brilliant circle of artists, writers, musicians, and scholars, entertaining them with music, dances, and games, as well as banquets and poetry readings. Cafaggiolo was also a place to breathe fresh air and hone the country skills required of gentlemen. By day Lorenzo might learn about the making of cheese and wine and at night study the constellations.

Cafaggiolo—country retreat, farm, fortress—lured Lorenzo de' Medici and his entourage from the city. The Flemish artist Giusto Utens painted this view of the Medici's favorite villa about 1599.

for the family's clothing and their beds boasted unparalleled magnificence. Abundant, delicate, but sumptuous jewelry—rings, bracelets, necklaces, brooches—adorned men and women alike.

But the new spirit reached outside the palace as well, to the villas surrounding it and to the Medici-financed convent of San Marco, where the walls shone brilliantly with frescoes by the Dominican friar Giovanni da Fiesole, known as Fra Angelico. A new kind of garden, more open and closer to nature, developed: vistas replaced the small, wall-enclosed world of the medieval garden; sculpture (often antique) adorned the paths; water splashed in fountains.

But the Medici held all these wonders in a tenuous grasp. They had as many enemies as friends, and for all their love of philosophy, the men of the Renaissance could be singularly ruthless. Assassinations, plots, intrigues, invasions all played their parts in contemporary politics. Any sign of Medici weakness attracted predators ready to exploit it. So, early on, Lorenzo needed to master the political skills necessary for success in such an environment. His father not only explained to him the intricate workings of the Florentine government and the Italian balance of power, but he also took him in as a junior partner. Consequently, when Piero died, Lorenzo was ready to take over as head of the family. At twenty Lorenzo assumed his place as one of the most powerful men in Europe.

Everything was quiet at first. An alliance among Naples, Florence, and Milan provided stability. The Florentine councils' favor weighed heavily toward the Medici. The city still prospered. But then, in 1471, trouble started. Florence looked to the neighboring city of Volterra for its supply of alum—an ore necessary to the dying of fabrics—and Volterra threatened to close off access to the mines. Lorenzo unhesitatingly behaved with the required ruthlessness. He ordered his army to attack Volterra, take it, sack it, and reduce it to unquestioning obedience.

Even so, political stability did not last for long. In 1471 a new pope, Sixtus IV, had been elected. In these days people almost expected the Holy Father to be greedy and self-seeking, but Sixtus exemplified these characteristics to an unusually high degree. A

TEXT CONTINUED ON PAGE 22

ROOTS OF THE RENAISSANCE

The glories of ancient Greece and Rome, rediscovered and romanticized by the Medici and other prominent families of fifteenth-century Florence, became those of the Renaissance, too. Feeding the Florentines' obsession with the classical world's pursuit of beauty and knowledge were new translations of Greek and Latin texts that celebrated mankind, nature, and worldly delights. The mania for antiquity sparked the collecting of long-lost artifacts, particularly Roman and Greek cameos and other carved stones. The Medici prized their antiques, which tell much of the Renaissance passion for the past—of gods and goddesses, muscular men, and voluptuous women.

Lorenzo de' Medici bought vases and cameos of jasper, onyx, agate, and sardonyx, adding to the collection begun by his grandfather Cosimo and his father, Piero. Lorenzo linked himself forever with the collection by having his name engraved on the finest pieces.

These treasures afforded Lorenzo an intimate pleasure. Hiding away the vases and cameos in cupboards, he preferred to admire their beauty in private. Alone with the classical shape of a vase or the evocative profile in a cameo, Lorenzo could contemplate the long-ago civilization that his own world so cherished.

Renaissance admirers of the serpent-handled ewer above saw in its shape the splendid past: the sardonyx jug is from the third or fourth century. Lorenzo had his name engraved around the vessel.

Lorenzo favored the jasper vase opposite for its antique style, though the lidded vessel is in fact Venetian. The gilt and enamel mounting is the work of Giusto da Firenze, a Florentine goldsmith who worked for the Medici.

BACCHUS DRIVING

GOD AND GODDESS OF THE SEA

Renaissance men were overnight archaeologists, scrambling for buried treasures—if possible, genuine cameos or engraved gems. Lorenzo's cameo collection, on this page and opposite, was superlative. Counterclockwise from top right, Poseidon and Amphitrite, god and goddess of the sea, rule their domain, while at left the wine god, Bacchus, drives his cart on an exquisite gem that may once have belonged to Mark Antony, the rival of the first Roman emperor, Augustus Caesar. At center Bacchus rides again, and below, Venus appears with her son Cupid; to their right Heracles shows a strong profile. In the broken cameo opposite, a satyr dances, and to his right, at top, Apollo, the god of light, plays for a satyr. Finally, Phaedra, princess of Crete, and her stepson appear in a complex engraving.

THE INFANT BACCHUS RIDES A BEAST

VENUS, CUPID, AND HERMAPHRODITUS

HERACLES IN PROFILE

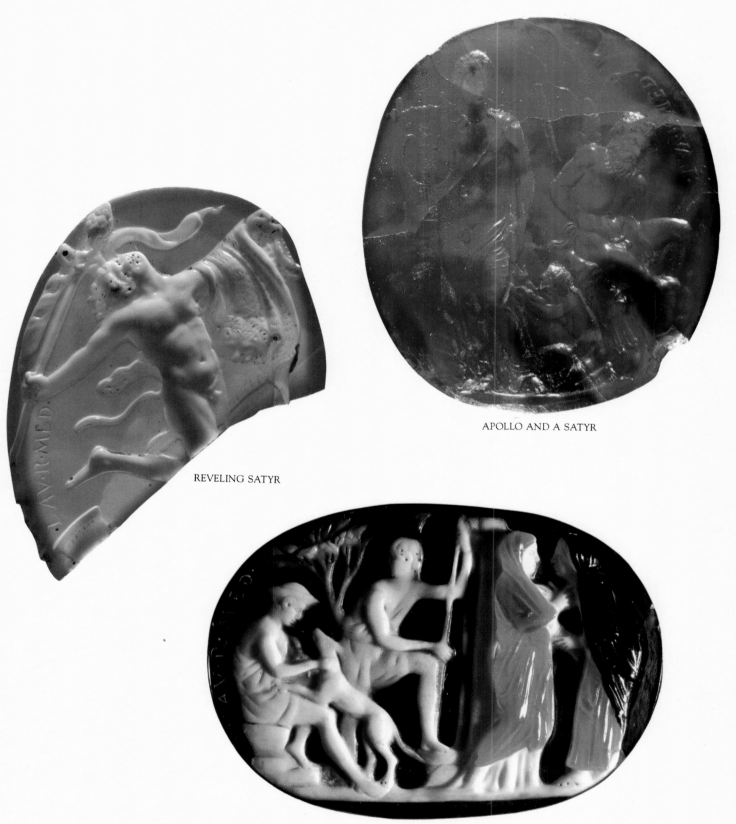

REVELING SATYR

APOLLO AND A SATYR

HIPPOLYTUS, A HUNTSMAN, PHAEDRA, A SERVANT

TEXT CONTINUED FROM PAGE 17

good family man, he fully intended to advance his nephew Girolamo Riario's career. But mere riches would not do for Girolamo. Sixtus was determined to find him a throne.

For several years the pope had been at odds with Lorenzo, who proved unwilling to cooperate in papal schemes. To be archbishop of Pisa, the pope had appointed a man whose corruption was extreme, even by the standards of the time. Seeing an opportunity to go against Sixtus, Lorenzo had refused to let the appointee take over the archdiocese. Further, the pope saw Lorenzo as a deterrent to the extention of the power of the Papal States. Lorenzo maintained a balance of power; once he vanished, the pope and his new ally, King Ferrante of Naples, might extend their sway indefinitely. Also, if the Medici could be removed from power, their fortune would become available to whoever eventually took over in Florence.

Since, for the sake of public opinion, the plot had to seem purely internal, the pope and his nephew got in touch with the Pazzi family, wealthy Florentine bankers who envied and resented the Medici. The Pazzi agreed to do most of the footwork; their reward would be dominance over Florence. Thus the scheme has gone down in history as the Pazzi conspiracy.

For the actual assassinations, their plan was simple. The pope and his nephew would remain in Rome while a member of the Pazzi family, Francesco, and the archbishop-designate of Pisa traveled to Florence on an ostensibly friendly visit. While there they would attend Mass one Sunday along with Lorenzo and his brother Giuliano and would murder them both in church. The day arrived and just as the Mass began, a disturbance erupted. Giuliano, across the cathedral from Lorenzo, found himself surrounded by men with drawn swords who attacked him with such fury that they eventually pierced his body with nineteen wounds. Two priests armed with daggers attacked Lorenzo, who had to defend himself.

Since he had hardly expected to be murdered at Mass, Lorenzo was at a disadvantage, but he drew his sword and fought, and soon his friends were able to surround him. Together they battled their way into the sacristy and slammed its bronze gates in their assailants'

In this grim drawing by Leonardo da Vinci—the great Florentine artist who was Lorenzo's protégé— an accomplice in the murder of Lorenzo's brother Giuliano meets justice by hanging. In Renaissance Florence, assassinations were commonplace.

THE PICTURE OF PERFECTION

Most Florentine women were poor in the fifteenth century. Some were slaves, and many lived as prostitutes. The Church offered one of the few real feminine careers. Nevertheless, a small number of courtesans and fortunate wives shared the luxuries and intellectual adventures of the day. Women lucky enough to wed wealth sometimes found themselves in the company of leisured, learned men eager to discuss literature, philosophy, and art. A few of these privileged brides—such as Simonetta Vespucci (at right), who married into the family of the famed navigator of the New World Amerigo Vespucci—won so much notice that their images appear in the work of renowned Renaissance artists. Even the Florentine master Sandro Botticelli may have modeled his portraits of mythical beauties on Simonetta.

Simonetta Vespucci embodied womanly perfection in her day. Her flawless milky complexion and light hair, as well as her curiosity and intelligence, impressed everyone upon her arrival in Florence, in 1475. Lorenzo's brother Giuliano pronounced Simonetta Queen of Beauty at a magnificent pageant. When the feast was over, Lorenzo described her effect on both men and women: "It seemed impossible that she was loved by so many men without any jealousy and praised by so many women without envy." Simonetta's origins enhanced her reputation, for she was born at the village on the Ligurian Sea called Portovenere, the legendary site of Venus' rising out of the water.

Though she died of tuberculosis at the age of twenty-three, Simonetta lived on in paintings and poems as the Renaissance ideal of the fashionable woman.

In a fanciful, posthumous portrait by the Florentine painter Piero di Cosimo, Simonetta Vespucci is oblivious to a snake around her neck as well as to the dark clouds behind her—images, perhaps, of an untimely death. With her brilliantly colored shawl and her hair in jeweled braids, she epitomizes cool elegance.

faces. From there Lorenzo, who did not yet know that his brother had been murdered, escaped safely to the Medici palace.

Several hours elapsed before he learned of the death of Giuliano—a young man, handsome and brilliant, of whom Lorenzo had been deeply fond. But the people of Florence had already rallied behind the Medici. By the end of the day, all but a few of the murderers had been caught and hanged, including the appointed archbishop of Pisa.

As soon as Sixtus found out that the plan had failed, he excommunicated Lorenzo and placed Florence under interdict: no Mass could be celebrated, no sacrament administered. The official reason he gave for these disciplinary measures was the execution of the archbishop-designate of Pisa. He fooled no one, least of all the king of Naples, who proceeded to implement stage two of the plan. The king sent troops to a valley sixty miles south of Florence. For the next two years war continued in a rather desultory way, as was then the custom. The Neapolitans won one battle but failed to take a little town that they besieged for several months. Nevertheless, Florence's position looked shaky, especially as her only ally, Milan, had been reduced to impotence by the murder of her duke a few years earlier.

But in 1479 a new duke of Milan—Lodovico Sforza—took over. When Lorenzo appealed to him for help, Lodovico advised trying for a reconciliation with Naples and added that he would use his influence with Ferrante; his sister had married Ferrante's son. In a gesture of incredible daring, Lorenzo left Florence secretly and sailed to Naples, gambling that his years of friendship with the notoriously treacherous Ferrante would guarantee his safety. When Lorenzo returned about three months later with a peace treaty, the Florentines received him as the savior of the city.

In that short time Lorenzo had proved himself the cleverest of Italian statesmen. Further, within a year Lorenzo had reorganized the government, creating an obedient new council called the Seventy, which would subjugate all others. On December 3, 1480, the pope, admitting defeat, received a Florentine embassy and lifted the interdict. Once again the old alliance of Milan, Florence, and

The Dominican monk Girolamo Savonarola, and two of his followers, hang on a burning stake in Florence's great square in 1498. Though Savonarola, with his fiery sermons opposing the tyranny and corruption of the Medici, developed a remarkable following, the Florentines eventually tired of his puritanism and turned against him.

Naples stabilized Italy; and this time Lorenzo could take full credit.

Although Lorenzo's political achievements were far-reaching, probably none alone would have done much for posterity's memory of him. In fact he founded his fame and that of Florence on the great cultural explosion he fostered. Most patrons simply bought paintings and sculptures; at best, they gave certain writers salaries. But Lorenzo, more than just generous, proved also to be accessible, interested, enthusiastic. Anyone, regardless of birth, could join his circle—made up of Ficino; the scholar-lecturer Angelo Poliziano, known as Politian; and Leon Battisti Alberti, the author of a key treatise on architecture—as its members discussed the nature of art, the best kind of government, the highest form of human development.

Such discussions and the resultant new opinions and ideas influenced the artists working in Florence; Sandro Botticelli, for example, translated Ficino's philosophy into paintings of genius. Botticelli's *Birth of Venus* and *Primavera* are works of incredible grace and beauty made more poignant by a touch of melancholy. The complex Neoplatonic symbols that make these works almost dissertations on the true nature of love have long been forgotten, but the paintings themselves remain masterpieces celebrating the rebirth of Florence under Lorenzo. Additionally, the artist known as Ghirlandajo produced portraits and paintings, in the guise of religious subjects, that showed the life-style of wealthy Florence. And under Andrea del Verrocchio's hand, sculpture reached a new degree of realism so that a bronze face seemed to breathe like that of its model.

Along with his support of the dazzling production of artworks, Lorenzo steadily and generously supported research and teaching. He founded a new university at Pisa and expanded the one at Florence—encouraging, in particular, the study of Greek. He also promoted the sciences. Some people believe that Lorenzo's workshop in the garden of San Marco constituted the first art academy—and was possibly the place where Lorenzo discovered the young Michelangelo modeling a bit of clay.

When Lorenzo died, in 1492, his eldest son, Piero, succeeded him as automatically as if Florence had been a kingdom instead of a republic. Another son, Giovanni, was already a cardinal—and would become Pope Leo X. The Medici moved their wealth from trade into real estate at an opportune moment, and Lorenzo's system seemed set to endure.

But without Lorenzo to keep the peace, the bickering rulers of Italy invited French intervention. Charles VIII appeared determined to reassert his rights over Naples, and in 1494 he invaded Italy. Piero, faced with the powerful French army, made an abject surrender, giving the king the right of passage through Florence as well as turning over to him the Florentine fortresses. Furious at this disgrace, the Florentines rebelled, and Piero and his brothers were forced to flee into exile.

Upon the Medici's departure a fanatical monk who had for several years been preaching against Lorenzo and the new hedonism seized the chance to gain influence over the Florentines, making use of the vacuum created by Piero's capitulation. The monk, Girolamo Savonarola, had gained notoriety some years before for his fiery sermons and his often uncanny predictions. Savonarola had actually forecasted Charles's invasion of Italy, and now he managed to convince the Florentines that Lorenzo and Piero had led them into a hedonistic, sinful way of life. From 1495 to 1498 the monk was the spiritual ruler of Florence, dominating the Florentine councils during the crisis that followed the Medici fall from favor. Savonarola urged the Florentines to change their sinful ways, and they followed him, turning away from the pleasure-seeking world of Lorenzo—a world that soon vanished.

Nevertheless, Lorenzo in his time had succeeded in his efforts to become Plato's philosopher-king incarnate. He had set a cultural example for other princes, who remembered him as Lorenzo the Magnificent. He had forever attached to his name an aura of discernment and intelligence, the aura of a prince whose treasures have transcendent value. Those fortunate enough to live in Florence and to be in Lorenzo's circle had experienced, in all its heady joys, the very spring of the Renaissance.

The Medici, particularly Lorenzo, helped make Florence the important city it was in the fifteenth century. Prominent families of the Renaissance could foster their material interests and glorify themselves by commissioning paintings by renowned artists of the day; and this the Medici did. The Florentine painters whose works appear on these pages—Benozzo Gozzoli, Paolo Uccello, and Sandro Botticelli—were in a sense as much the treasured possessions of the family as were their paintings. One of the pleasures of patronage, of course, was to be able to afford the best painters of the day. Though the artists, in theory at least, were free to paint as they chose, their benefactors often dictated the subject of the paintings, and the likenesses of the patrons often figured in the paintings. The Medici wanted these works not simply for their beauty and the technical skill the painters displayed, but for the political and ideological significance of the subject matter.

The frescoes and painters here commemorate three abiding concerns of the Medici. First, the family saw its public role as similar to that of the Magi, the three kings who brought gifts to the infant Christ. In annual biblical pageants that took place in the public square, the Medici dressed as the Magi to celebrate Epiphany, the observance of the Magi's journey. Such fanfare not only provided excellent subject matter for paintings, but also called attention to the Medici's lavish support of the Church. Both painting and pageant confirmed the special status the family claimed for itself in Florence.

The city itself was another family obsession, and the Medici ordered works that immortalized the history, beauty, and might of their beloved Florence. Finally, the Medici were among the leading proponents of classical learning in their time. They encouraged the study of ancient Greece and Rome: Lorenzo delighted in recognizing classical references. In pictures the Medici could honor the gods and goddesses of classical mythology just as easily as they could put themselves in the company of Christ.

Much of what the Medici commissioned was public property, but even when the art went into their palaces and private chapels, the meaning of the pictures was not restricted to an exclusive audience. The natural beauty, skill, intellectual curiosity, and optimism conveyed in these images touched every proud Florentine.

In 1439 the emperor of the Eastern Roman Empire, John Paleologus (opposite), celebrated Epiphany with the Medici in the streets of Florence. Paleologus, who had come from his capital, Constantinople, with his circle of classical scholars, joined the cavalcade as one of the three kings. With his beard, turban, and black-and-gold robe, Paleologus cut an exotic figure, yet the emperor's opulently caparisoned horse nearly outshone its rider. The Medici commissioned artist Benozzo Gozzoli to record the event in a series of frescoes for the family's chapel. Other details are on pages 30–33.

OVERLEAF: The Magi and their grand retinue wend their way down craggy, imaginary terrain. Gozzoli made distinctive portraits of many participants in the make-believe journey, paying attention to each man's costume and to the horses' elaborate harnesses. Young guards, armed with spears, swords, and bows and arrows, walk next to the parade's dignitaries, who include members of the Medici family. The youth at right holds a golden offering, as one of the three wise men did for Christ.

Benozzo Gozzoli, his name circling his red cap, rides behind the Medici clan in another detail from the frescoes he painted for the family's chapel. Unlike the clean-shaven Florentines, some men who accompanied Emperor Paleologus (see page 28) to the Magi pageant sport beards—in a city where facial hair was considered barbarian. Whatever their differences in style and custom, the turbaned, crowned, and capped crowd moved as one in the procession.

The curly haired boy opposite, playing one of the Magi in Gozzoli's fresco, may be an idealized portrait of Lorenzo de' Medici. The leaves framing the young king give a clue to his identity, since the Latin name for laurel, laurus, would be his namesake as well. In a gold damask coat and an ornamented Florentine hat called a mazzocchio, the youth is perhaps the most richly attired in the procession.

lances, swords, and hammers. The battleground, littered with broken lances and lost armor, is a grim contrast to the bucolic background.

A high-hatted Niccolò da Tolentino drives on against the strong Sienese, as the helmeted soldiers of fortune have at each other wit

Generals were for hire in fifteenth-century Italy. Called condottieri, they conducted the wars declared by rich and powerful men such as the Medici, who did their best to steer clear of the fray. Skilled soldiers and generals, and the men who hired them, looked upon fighting as the ultimate game. Paolo Uccello's three very large paintings collectively called the *Rout of San Romano* (the first painting here and the remaining two in the foldout) celebrate Florence's victory over powerful Siena in a minor battle in 1432—and show war as the elaborate tournament that Renaissance men fancied it to be. Cosimo de' Medici probably commissioned the paintings in honor of Condottiere Niccolò da Tolentino, who won the battle for Florence.

Uccello's three panels, their total length exceeding thirty-four feet, filled one end of a bedroom in the Medici palace occupied first by Piero, then Lorenzo. Both father and son delighted in the artist's strong yet playful images of sportsmanship, gallantry, and derring-do. Each painting glorifies the Florentines: the outnumbered soldiers rallying around Niccolò, a general arriving with reinforcements, a mounted soldier knocking the Sienese leader off his horse.

Rout of San Romano did not show the Medici what actually happened in 1432—but told a romantic story of fighting for the virtue of Florence. Looking at Uccello's paintings, Lorenzo could relish the art of war—at a comfortable distance from the bloody battlefield.

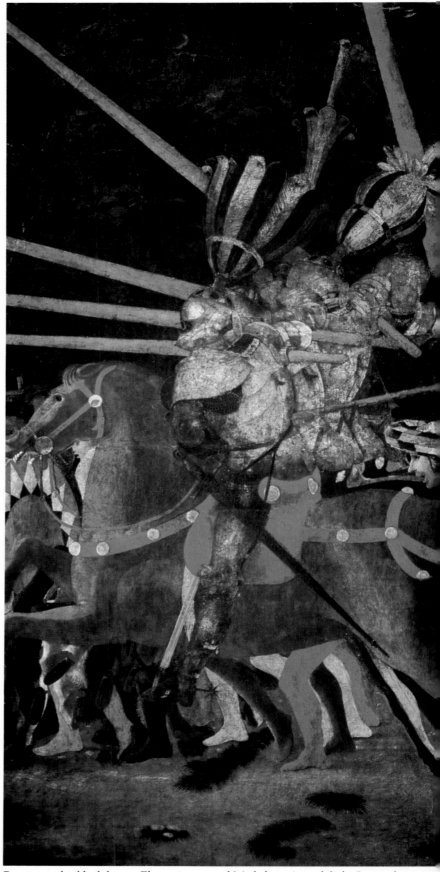

Rearing on his black horse, Florentine general Micheletto Attendoli da Cotignola

FOLDOUT ⟶

saves the day with his counterattack at San Romano. When the replacements arrived the Florentines finally beat off the Sienese.

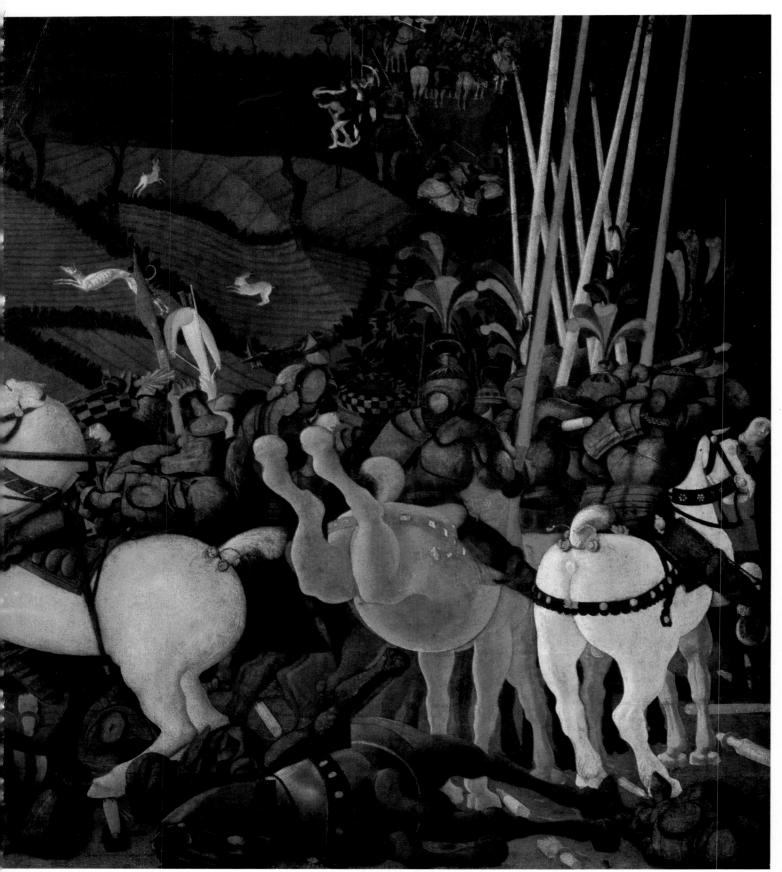

the battle of San Romano. Weary troops retreat toward hills where a hound, mimicking the aggressive Florentines, scatters hares.

In the midst of crossbows and plumes—and trampling fallen steeds and riders—a Florentine mercenary unhorses the Sienese leader, winning

In Sandro Botticelli's painting Adoration of the Magi, *above, the Medici gather under a rustic but majestic shelter: Cosimo holds the Christ Child's feet; Piero in a red cloak kneels below the Virgin Mary; Giuliano is to the right of him; and the young Lorenzo with his sword stands at left. Botticelli, confidently including himself in the Medici's inner circle, gazes out in a self-portrait in the foreground at far right. The lordly, elegantly robed congregation, all intimates of the Medici family, takes little notice of the holy occasion. In the detail opposite, the diffident Lorenzo ignores a friend's embrace and an affectionate horse. Giovanni del Lama, a Florentine merchant, commissioned the painting about 1475.*

Botticelli's fascination with the ancient world and its pagan images fills his paintings on these and the following two pages. In Birth of Venus, *at left*, wind gods blow ashore a seashell on which stands the goddess of love. A robed woman offers the nude Venus a flowered wrap; the showers of roses and blossoms on the garments suggest spring. Lorenzo di Pierfrancesco, a Medici cousin, commissioned the painting—perhaps to prove himself a devotee of the philosophy of the time, a mixture of classical mythology and Christian teachings.

OVERLEAF: *Botticelli's* Primavera, *or "Spring," is a tangle of mythological stories, with—from the left— the god of science and commerce, Mercury; a trio of lovely women personifying beauty, grace, and charm; Venus; a woman personifying spring; the nymph Chloris; and the wind god Zephyr all meeting in an orange grove. Though the intentions of the artist—and those of his Medici patron, Lorenzo di Pierfrancesco—are unknown, the painting is a joyous allegory of spring and love. Both* Primavera *and* Birth of Venus *hung in the villa of Pierfrancesco, where they gloriously illustrated—with nearly life-size figures—the philosophical interests of a cultivated, late fifteenth-century Florentine.*

II

ISABELLA D'ESTE

LA PRIMA DONNA DEL MONDO

Ferrara in the last quarter of the fifteenth century was just a small city in northern Italy, but there, too, the Renaissance was in bloom. Sumptuous tapestries, rich fabrics, paintings by such great contemporary masters as Cosimo Tura and Andrea Mantegna decorated the walls of the palace. Precious objects abounded. The duke's collection of gold, silver, and bronze medals, both ancient and modern, was as famous as his library. Besides being an efficient ruler, Duke Ercole d'Este was a scholar and a booklover. The Roman historian Quintus Curcius was first translated into Italian at his order, and his taste ranged from Greek authors and such classic Italian masterpieces as the love sonnets of Francesco Petrarca—or Petrarch—to the most experimental Italian writers of his day.

Incredibly enough, the little states of Italy, whose dominion encompassed only a few dozen square miles, actually played a major political role: in the fifteenth century size was not all. Because the balance of power was so fragile, even very small states mattered. By hiring themselves out to Venice, or Florence, or Milan, they could

---

Isabella d'Este—who in 1534, at sixty, had herself portrayed as the young woman opposite—was an art patron and, as marchesa of Mantua, a formidable ruler.

make the difference between victory and defeat. Still, their territories remained a standing temptation to their larger neighbors, so they had to be constantly on the defensive in order to survive.

That the court of Ferrara was so splendid reflected its ruler's love of pleasure; but luxury played a crucial political role as well. The conspicuous display of wealth showed that the state had all the resources it needed to defend itself, and that, no matter how small the dukedom, its ruler was just as good, as sophisticated, as important as his bigger neighbors. And so, although Duke Ercole enjoyed all of his palaces and his villas—including the Palazzo di Schifanoia where frescoes were framed in carved marble—he was also making a serious political statement by owning such treasure-houses.

In 1474, in the midst of all this splendor, Isabella d'Este was born, and within a year so was her sister Beatrice. Because the duke was a modern-minded ruler, he treated both girls as if they were boys: he never thought of curtailing their education because of their sex.

Along with her book learning, Isabella also learned that danger was always close. In 1476, at the age of two, she was awakened in the middle of the night and bundled off in haste along a covered gallery to a fortress. Niccolò d'Este, her father's cousin, had been plotting to replace Ercole. Niccolò failed and was beheaded along with twenty-five of his accomplices. When Isabella was only eight years old, Venice invaded her father's duchy, and the little girls were sent off to Modena. They stayed there for two years as their father desperately fought to retain his realm. Even when the duke managed to arrange a peace in 1484, no one thought it likely to last.

Amid the turmoil Isabella learned Greek, Latin, and classical literature and studied Ficino's writings as well as other works that represented the latest trends in philosophy. She learned to dance, to sing, to play music, to dress well, and to act graciously. She learned to accompany her songs on the lute in front of the entire court, and with her wavy blond hair, dark blue eyes, and delicate complexion, she looked enchanting. The little girl was also eager and bright. She had the understanding and the skills necessary for one who would, some day, have a court of her own. And she learned more than

In the streets of Mantua, a faction of the Bonacolsi family, on the right, clashes with troops of the Gonzaga family, who expelled the Bonacolsi and seized control of the city in 1328. This painting commemorating the event was made more than 160 years later for Francesco Gonzaga, the fourth Gonzaga marchese and husband of Isabella d'Este.

merely how to be gracious; by the time she was sixteen, she could converse as an equal with Lodovico Ariosto, the author of the great, fantastical epic poem, *Orlando Furioso*. One of her cousins pronounced her "the first lady of the world"—*la prima donna del mondo*—and that assessment, exalted as it was, surprised no one.

Given the circumstances of her birth, Isabella inevitably became a pawn in Italy's diplomatic game. At the age of six, she was betrothed to Francesco Gonzaga, the heir to neighboring Mantua, while Beatrice was slated to marry the duke of Milan. When Francesco, at the age of twenty-four, succeeded his father as marchese, the time for the wedding had clearly come. Isabella, not quite sixteen, was an adult by the standards of the time. Francesco duly set out for Ferrara to claim his fiancée. There he found that he had not only gained an ally, but was also about to marry an exceptionally bright and appealing young woman. As for Isabella, she saw a short, dark, ugly, young man with frizzy hair and a face a little like a pug's; but he was athletic and full of charm, and the political alliance quickly became a love match.

The wedding celebrations were splendid. The best goldsmith in Milan made a belt, buttons, and seals for Isabella out of gold and silver; her presents came in the finest chests; her dresses were made of the most spectacular, most expensive brocade. At the great banquet the walls were hung with a set of the Este family's tapestries, embroidered in gold and silver thread and decorated with pearls. A special set of gold and silver dishes supported by dragons, satyrs, and dolphins came from Venice. The drinking cups were made of solid gold. Plays and balls were staged. In the very midst of the heady mix of romance and politics, the bridegroom signed a contract with the Venetians, who hired him to lead his army on Venice's behalf. The young couple left Ferrara and floated down the Po to Mantua in a gilded barge, followed by fifty scarlet boats bearing the court with its musicians and poets—a triumphal wedding trip.

The reception in Mantua was as spectacular as the send-off from Ferrara had been. Wine took the place of water in the city's fountains. The townspeople participated in processions, concerts, and

TEXT CONTINUED ON PAGE 56

A ceiling painted to simulate a dome, open at the center and decorated with busts of Roman emperors, looms above the frescoed walls of the Camera Picta. Beside the entrance are scenes, in detail opposite and on pages 52–53, of Lodovico Gonzaga, his family, and his court.

THE CAMERA PICTA

Once the Gonzaga firmly established themselves in Mantua, they sought permanent symbols of their wealth and prestige. The finest tribute was commissioned by the second marchese, Lodovico, probably the most gifted of the Gonzaga princes. One of his achievements was to persuade Andrea Mantegna, a highly renowned artist in northern Italy, to become his court painter. In 1465, shortly after settling in Mantua, Mantegna began a series of frescoes at the family's Palazzo Ducale, in a tower room known as the Camera Picta, or "Painted Chamber." This small, square space, which is about eight yards long on each side, may once have been a bedroom—it has also been known as the bridal chamber—but was more likely used for holding audiences and storing precious objects.

Mantegna spent nine years on the project, finishing the room in 1474, the year that Isabella d'Este was born. The surviving frescoes, shown in detail here and on pages 52–55, include a marvelous, illusionistic ceiling and many magnificent—if not always flattering—family portraits. Completely secular in content, the portraits splendidly convey the dynastic character of the Gonzaga house at a time when princely families throughout Italy had come to rival the Church in pomp and power.

The young Francesco stands to the left of his brother Sigismondo, a future cardinal. Behind the two boys towers the robed figure—partially visible in this detail—of their uncle Francesco, who had been made a cardinal in 1461.

Exuding dignity and authority, members of the Gonzaga family and court assemble on a terrace. The marchese Lodovico, seated at far left, turns to confer with his secretary, as his wife, Barbara of Brandenburg, looks on expectantly. Kneeling between the couple, with a piece of fruit in her hand, is their youngest daughter. Other children, pages, courtiers, and a dwarf—who functioned as a jester and companion—stand behind and to the right, and a favorite dog crouches under Lodovico's chair.

53

Court ladies, a turbaned slave, and several cupids with a peacock in their midst lean over a circular balustrade that opens to the sky.

This decorative illusion, painted on the vault of the ceiling, was among the most enchanting features for visitors to the Camera Picta.

TEXT CONTINUED FROM PAGE 49

banquets. In the years that followed the wedding celebrations, Isabella did her best to sustain the tone that had been set. She surrounded herself with jesters and dwarfs (for whom she had a particular taste) and stylish ladies-in-waiting. For her own personal use in the palace, she selected a room with a view of the lake and had the room redone with blue-and-gold ceilings and inlaid wall paneling. She made the room a blend of study, studio, and living room—a so-called *studiolo*.

She gathered books and precious objects and paintings and began to add to these collections new objects that she bought or commissioned herself. "I want engraved amethysts," she wrote to one of her agents, "rosaries of gold and black amber, blue cloth for a vest, black cloth for a coat which must be of unequalled splendor. Even if it should cost ten ducats an ell, do not spare the money so long as it is really magnificent. I would rather do without it than risk seeing a similar coat on someone else."

Her library contained very little when she arrived. Aldus Manutius, a great printer and classical scholar who settled in Venice, was then putting out new, crisply designed editions of Aristotle and Plato, which he and some of the brightest young scholars of the day edited. Aldus's printshop became one of the leading intellectual centers of the Renaissance, and Isabella ordered quantities of books from the Aldine Press. Not simply intent on getting the very latest books, Isabella also insisted that Aldus use the best paper available and bind her copies in green leather with gold.

Isabella soon proved that she was fully capable of looking after political matters. At first she simply kept up with Mantua's many alliances. When her sister Beatrice married Lodovico Sforza, the duke of Milan, Isabella went to the wedding and made a great impression, not least because of her splendid clothes. Shortly before her trip, for instance, she ordered over seventy sable skins to trim a coat lined in crimson satin. She could not have afforded to look less dazzling than Beatrice for then people would have assumed that Mantua was a second-rate power. In 1493 she made still another contribution to the interests of the Gonzaga family by presenting

Portraits of two favorite racehorses belonging to Federico Gonzaga, Isabella's oldest son, adorn a frescoed wall at the Palazzo del Tè, the family's pleasure pavilion on an island outside Mantua. Both Federico and his father excelled at horse breeding, and Gonzaga steeds were prized as gifts in all the courts throughout Europe.

Francesco with a daughter. Five more children would follow.

About this time Italian politics—never simple—became even more complicated. In 1492 Cardinal Rodrigo Borgia had been elected to the pontifical throne, and, as Alexander VI, he promptly set a record for greed, debauchery, and ruthlessness. He allowed nothing to stop him or even slow him down in his quest for power. He had two grown children, Cesare and Lucrezia, and together the three Borgia acquired a reputation for betraying and poisoning opponents that won them a kind of immortality.

Two years after Alexander became pope, King Charles VIII of France decided to enforce his claim to Naples and marched into Italy at the head of a powerful army. With the agreement of a series of very nervous rulers, he proceeded unchecked down the peninsula. In Florence the insurrection that chased out the Medici threw the whole of central Italy up for grabs. The fragile equilibrium so painstakingly maintained by Lorenzo the Magnificent was shattered; for the next fifty years the pattern of wars, rebellions, conquests, and treachery shifted with bewildering complexity, so that even the most astute of statesmen had trouble deciding what to do next.

The smaller Italian states felt themselves to be particularly endangered. In Mantua Francesco Gonzaga, who was a brave, competent soldier, proved less adept as a politician, and the survival of Mantua came increasingly to depend on Isabella. She turned first to Lodovico Sforza because Milan was rich and Lodovico was a formidable general. An alliance between Mantua and Milan developed naturally, and Isabella worked hard at keeping the Sforza family happy, while impressing on Francesco, who disliked them, that he had to court their favor. So intent was Isabella on the success of this policy that when Francesco went to Milan to discuss hiring himself and his troops to the duke, she actually pawned her jewels in order to get him the proper clothes.

Soon Mantua joined the new anti-French league of Milan, Rome, Venice, and Spain. Francesco assumed command of the allied armies, and, in 1495, at Fornovo di Taro, largely through chance, he managed to defeat the French. Immediately Mantuan prestige rose.

IL LIBRO
DEL CORTEGIANO
DEL CONTE BALDESAR
CASTIGLIONE,
NVOVAMENTE STAMPATO,
*Et con somma diligenza
reuisto.*

VIVO MORTE,
RESPECTA MEA.

IN VENETIA PER CABRIEL
IOLITO DE FERRARII.
M. D. XXXXI.

THE GENTLEMAN'S HANDBOOK

Baldassare Castiglione (above), portrayed in about 1515 by his friend Raffaello Santi, the great painter known as Raphael, displays the elegance and inner calm that he extolled as gentlemanly ideals in The Book of the Courtier. *Castiglione's own career at the court of Urbino inspired his influential work, which he published in 1528. The 1541 edition (at left) was one of more than sixty Italian editions that appeared, along with many foreign translations, by the end of the century.*

Even as they patronized the fine arts, Renaissance aristocrats were increasingly preoccupied with the art of living. In an open, richly varied society, where the conditions of accceptance were changing, the newly rich put a premium on being considered true gentlemen. Out of this search for respectability grew a huge literature devoted to proper conduct. The most famous guide was Baldassare Castiglione's *The Book of the Courtier.*

A scholar and diplomat from Mantua, Castiglione served Francesco Gonzaga and his wife, Isabella, from 1489 to 1504. He next moved to the nearby court of Urbino, then ruled by Guido Ubaldo da Montefeltro and his wife, Elisabetta, Isabella's sister-in-law. Many notable guests gathered regularly at the palace, and in 1507 Castiglione began setting down their conversations in a book, where he had the participants attempt to define the attributes of the perfect courtier.

The knightly qualities of courage and honor were deemed prime virtues, along with skill at arms, swimming, running, and playing tennis. A gentleman must also be quick in conversation, humorous but never crude, learned but never stuffy. Dancing was a proper pastime, and so, too, was the pursuit of love (though not lust). Above all the courtier must affect *sprezzatura,* or "nonchalance," "so as...to make whatever is done or said appear to be without effort...."

The picture of court life offered in *The Courtier,* while charming, was of course extremely one-sided. Certainly there were gentlemen who embraced Castiglione's standards. Yet his book was written against a background of violence, and Italy's princes, however refined they may have acted in public, were privately often vulgar and murderous. Nevertheless, the image created by Castiglione endured: his book was a great success, and for many years it made Italian courts synonymous with elegant, sophisticated living.

Venice gave Francesco a two-thousand-ducat raise and made him captain-general of her forces, while Isabella received as her share of the booty the magnificent tapestries that had adorned Charles VIII's tent. And as soon as Francesco came home, she commissioned Mantegna to record the victory in a painting, which she donated to a newly built church.

Two years later, however, the Venetians fired Francesco for becoming too friendly with the French. Mantua's fortunes changed again. Once more Isabella turned to Milan for employment for Francesco and his army. In July 1498 Beatrice died in childbirth, and Francesco paid a visit to Milan, ostensibly a condolence call on Lodovico. Nothing came of his trip, and so Isabella took a more direct hand. She asked Lodovico to send an embassy to her in Mantua, and there she gave a series of magnificent entertainments for the Milanese and convinced them at last to hire Francesco at the huge salary of forty thousand ducats a year.

No sooner had Isabella settled her alliance with Lodovico than Charles VIII died, and the new French king, Louis XII, reinvaded Italy with another formidable army. On Isabella's advice, Francesco switched sides and joined the French. When the battle came the Mantuan troops stayed well away from it and so ensured Lodovico's defeat. Without a moment's hesitation Isabella gave refuge to the vanquished duke and treated him well—while simultaneously negotiating an alliance with France, visiting the new ruler who replaced Lodovico, and returning to Mantua with her very own booty.

Next the Borgia threatened Isabella. Alexander VI, however evil his reputation, was a practical man who wanted to see Italy united under his son Cesare. With the pope's backing and by ruse, treachery, and murder, Cesare took town after town and made himself the most powerful man in the peninsula, dispossessing several of Isabella's relatives along the way. Isabella kept her feelings to herself and courted Cesare so as to protect herself from his ambition. As a result Alexander VI suggested a marriage between his daughter Lucrezia and Isabella's brother Alfonso.

Isabella—although she was privately horrified—rejoiced pub-

Hounds leap upon a wild boar pursued by a mounted huntsman in this detail of a wall painting from the Gonzaga's Palazzo del Tè. Sometimes two thousand nobles, servants, and hangers-on took part in a hunt; and beaters equipped with sticks—like the boy above portrayed in classical garb—would drive out boars, deer, rabbits, and goats for the kill.

licly. She was aware, of course, that Lucrezia had divorced one husband and murdered the next, hardly a promising precedent, but nevertheless at the wedding ceremonies Isabella dazzled everybody. One night she wore a black velvet dress adorned with lynx, a green velvet coat sewn with gold plaques, a gold crown, and several diamond necklaces. Another night her dress was made of crimson satin and black velvet with a massive gold, ruby, and pearl belt. Even Lucrezia, always fashion-conscious, was impressed. And because Francesco, as usual, was talking too much, Isabella wrote him, on July 23, 1502, "I hear...that your Excellency has spoken ill of [Cesare]...in the presence of [Louis XII] and people belonging to the Pope. Whether this rumor be true or false, it will reach the ears of [Cesare]...who will not hesitate to plot against you." Since the Borgia had the unsavory reputation of using poison often and effectively, she cautioned her husband about eating anything that had not been tasted first.

Before long, though, Isabella actually consented to the betrothal of her infant daughter to Cesare's son—and in the arrangements remembered to claim some antique statuary that Cesare had seized when he took Urbino. In 1503, however, when Alexander VI died, the match was off. Then, within the year, Cesare's fortunes changed. He ended up in prison, and the Borgia's power quickly became just a memory. Isabella, on the other hand, went on ruling. "Ask Madama," Francesco would say whenever a problem came up; the marriage between Francesco and Isabella soon transformed itself into a thoroughly businesslike relationship.

Francesco had mistresses, whom he chose from among the ladies of Ferrara, and Isabella knew all about them. But when the need arose to defend Mantua, Isabella and Francesco behaved like the most united of couples, as their cooperation became more essential than ever. France fought Spain, and aggressive popes tried to extend their domains. In 1509 the Venetians took Francesco prisoner and announced that they planned to keep him for good. During his captivity Isabella ruled entirely on her own. "Everything is referred to Madama," wrote one of her envoys, "and not a leaf stirs without her consent." Eventually, with the help of the pope, Isabella got her husband back. But Francesco had contracted syphilis, which was then incurable, and so he moved into a country villa and left the government to her. From then on, until his death in 1519, she carried on her dangerous task with ruthless realism.

At the same time no problems could stop her from enjoying life. She installed herself in a new suite of sixteen rooms and called it her Paradiso—her "paradise." There she gathered all her collections. The doorframes were made of carved marble. Mosaics and sculptures filled a grotto, and, since she assiduously bought paintings from the best living artists, she amassed a world-famous collection. Eventually, a century later, Charles I of England bought it.

Isabella's fame rested, however, not just on the way she dressed, decorated her palace, or accumulated treasures. Rather, she drew others to her with her open, lively intelligence, her humor, and her zest for life. She surrounded herself with intellectuals such as Mario Equicola, a leading scholar, and Baldassare Castiglione, whose book *The Courtier* defined the right dress, manners, pastimes, and very spirit of the modern Renaissance gentleman and gentlewoman. Isabella corresponded widely with members of her family, other rulers, and her agents everywhere. She aided and encouraged Ariosto. She patronized the newest, most daring painters, kept first-rate musicians, and made Mantua one of the great intellectual centers of the Renaissance.

The only restraint on Isabella's appetite for the rare and the beautiful was the size of her income. Throughout her life she complained about insufficient funds. Again and again she pawned her jewels, borrowing everywhere. Still she managed to keep herself surrounded by her dwarfs, who were highly collectible items. She always had a troupe of dogs. On the walls hung her many portraits, including one of her drawn by the great artist Leonardo da Vinci. She bought cameos, medals, rare glass objects, oriental fabrics. She had a special collection of musical instruments. Her jewels were dazzling. And finally even her dishes were the finest majolica ware, each piece adorned with a different scene from classical myth-

In another Palazzo del Tè scene that celebrates the princely passion for hunting, an archer takes aim at a flock of geese with a crossbow—a weapon that was beginning to replace the hawks used since the Middle Ages. Hunts were often a part of pageants, and on such occasions ladies would watch from a hillside as their men closed in on the game.

ology or the Bible, all with her coat of arms prominently displayed.

For a while, after Francesco's death and the accession of her son Federico, she went on ruling Mantua; but then Federico set up his mistress as a rival to his mother. Little by little, Isabella saw her court dwindle; in 1520 she packed up her collections and moved to Rome. Isabella promptly established herself as one of Rome's luminaries and persuaded the pope to make her younger son a cardinal. Even away from home, she never forgot politics.

Her acumen in backing the Spanish, and not the French, saw her safely through the sack of Rome in 1527. The pope, in alliance with France, had been undermining Emperor Charles V's power. So the emperor, although an ardent Catholic himself, allowed his army, composed mostly of Swiss and German mercenaries, to move down the peninsula and lay siege to Rome. The emperor's army breached the city's walls, and troops spread throughout the city, looting and raping. Fortunately one of the emperor's generals happened to be Isabella's son; the only secure place in Rome was Isabella's palace, to which she had admitted over a thousand refugees.

Three years after the sack of Rome, a chastened pope acknowledged Charles's victory by formally crowning him Holy Roman Emperor at Bologna. At the coronation Isabella staged her last—and greatest—triumph. Making herself the center of great occasions had long ago become Isabella's specialty. Once again she was splendidly dressed, admirably fashionable, and shining with intelligence. She had established herself, too, as one of the mainstays of the Spanish party. The emperor not only noticed her, but, after a conversation with her, he announced that he would soon visit Mantua. In Mantua Isabella put on yet another grand reception, and, on the steps of the cathedral, the emperor announced that henceforth the ruler of Mantua would be not a marchese, but a duke.

Although Isabella may have been at odds with her son, she cared a great deal about her dynasty. Now she had not only ensured the survival of her city but had raised it to a higher level politically. She was indeed the first lady of her times, and under her sway she nurtured the flowering of the Renaissance.

A CRAZE FOR THE ANTIQUE

This bronze vase by Antico, Isabella's favorite sculptor, who won his name reworking Greek and Roman art, bears a processional frieze near the base of the bowl.

"One large cameo set in gold," is the first item on this inventory of Isabella's grotta and other rooms. Altogether the list includes 1,620 objects.

The marriage in 1490 of Isabella d'Este to Francesco Gonzaga united a woman hungry for art, as she once confessed, with a family that had been patrons of the finest artists and their works for two centuries. In such a receptive environment, Isabella lost no time creating her own private treasure chest within her apartments at Mantua's Palazzo Ducale. Almost at once she prepared a *studiolo*—a small room for housing books, manuscripts, and musical instruments. Most cultivated princes of the Renaissance had studioli, and Isabella decorated hers with paintings, carved and gilded woodwork, and marble inlays on the door.

Equally splendid was a cavernous room that was known as the *grotta* because of its vaulted ceiling and its position directly under the studiolo. Here Isabella indulged what amounted to an obsession with antiquities. She was no purist: she valued not only Greek and Roman art, but also contemporary works in the classical style. Her special love was sculpture, partly because

possessing it carried prestige. And she acquired ceramics and medallions as well—anything with an ancient theme delighted her.

For her, and for several generations of Gonzaga, no one better mastered the skill at recreating the classical than the sculptor Pier Jacopo Alari-Bonacolsi, nicknamed Antico. Trained as a goldsmith, Antico soon turned to bronze, and in 1497 Francesco Gonzaga sent Antico to Rome to study the masterpieces of antique statuary. These he reinterpreted brilliantly on a smaller scale, producing statuettes and other decorative pieces famed for their expressiveness, firm line, and perfect finish. Of the Antico works on pages 66–71, some were commissioned by Isabella, others by Gonzaga men—though Isabella may well have ultimately acquired them for herself. The gleaming objects crowded the shelves and ledges of the grotta, where their owner could discuss and admire them and—for special pleasure—take them down and hold them in her hands.

Inside a frame of diamonds and enamel, a Latin inscription denoting Isabella as the marchesa of Mantua surrounds her profile on the gold medal opposite. Isabella displayed this piece in her grotta, and she also sent medals to her admirers.

A superb thirteen-inch-high bronze statuette of
Venus, in four views, epitomizes what Antico
achieved in interpreting an antique work for his
Gonzaga patrons. The sculptor based his Venus on
an over-life-size marble statue in Rome. But he
transformed that matronly version of the Roman
goddess into an aristocratic, up-to-date beauty, en-
nobled with gilt robes and hair.

The Gonzaga commissioned several versions of this splendid Apollo, here displaying his gilded hair and cloak. Antico adapted the statuette from a classical marble known as the Apollo Belvedere—the most famous ancient sculpture of the Renaissance.

A bust of Bacchus (above) has a sumptuous patina that, like the finish on most Renaissance bronzes, emulated what artists assumed was the original condition of ancient bronzes. Isabella most likely placed this bust in her grotta alongside the partly gilded bust (right) portraying Ariadne, the wife of Bacchus.

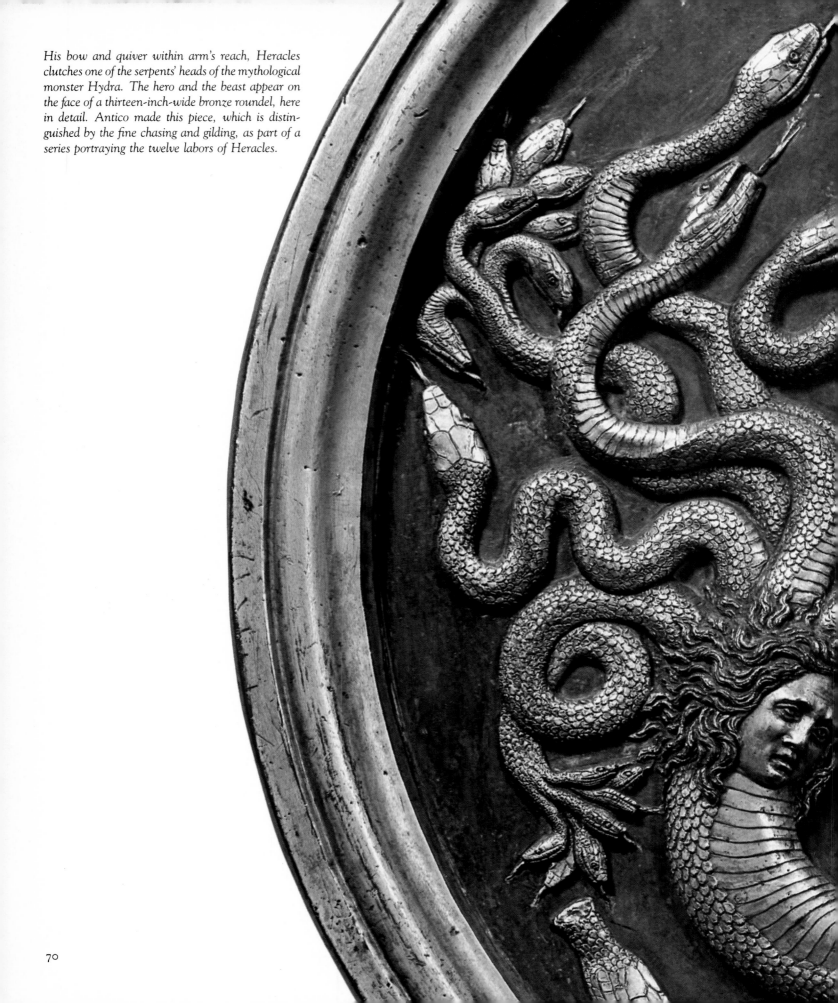

His bow and quiver within arm's reach, Heracles clutches one of the serpents' heads of the mythological monster Hydra. The hero and the beast appear on the face of a thirteen-inch-wide bronze roundel, here in detail. Antico made this piece, which is distinguished by the fine chasing and gilding, as part of a series portraying the twelve labors of Heracles.

About 1525 Isabella acquired a set of brilliantly painted majolica plates, so called after the island of Majorca, where majolica ware originated. Isabella's dishes, like all her possessions, were chiefly for display, though she may actually have used them at table on grand occasions. The three plates here bear Gonzaga and Este arms and scenes from classical myth. On the plate at right, the Greek hero Peleus chases the goddess Thetis, who coyly changes into a bird and a dragon. Below, the sun god Apollo, having slain a monster, sets off in pursuit of a nymph. Opposite, the Roman emperor Trajan halts his army to hear a mother's pleas. Gonzaga arms adorn the tower in the background.

PELEUS PURSUES HIS LOVE

APOLLO AT WORK AND PLAY

THE MERCIFUL EMPEROR

OVERLEAF: *In this detail from the plate above,
Trajan listens to the tale of a grieving mother
whose son has been slain.*

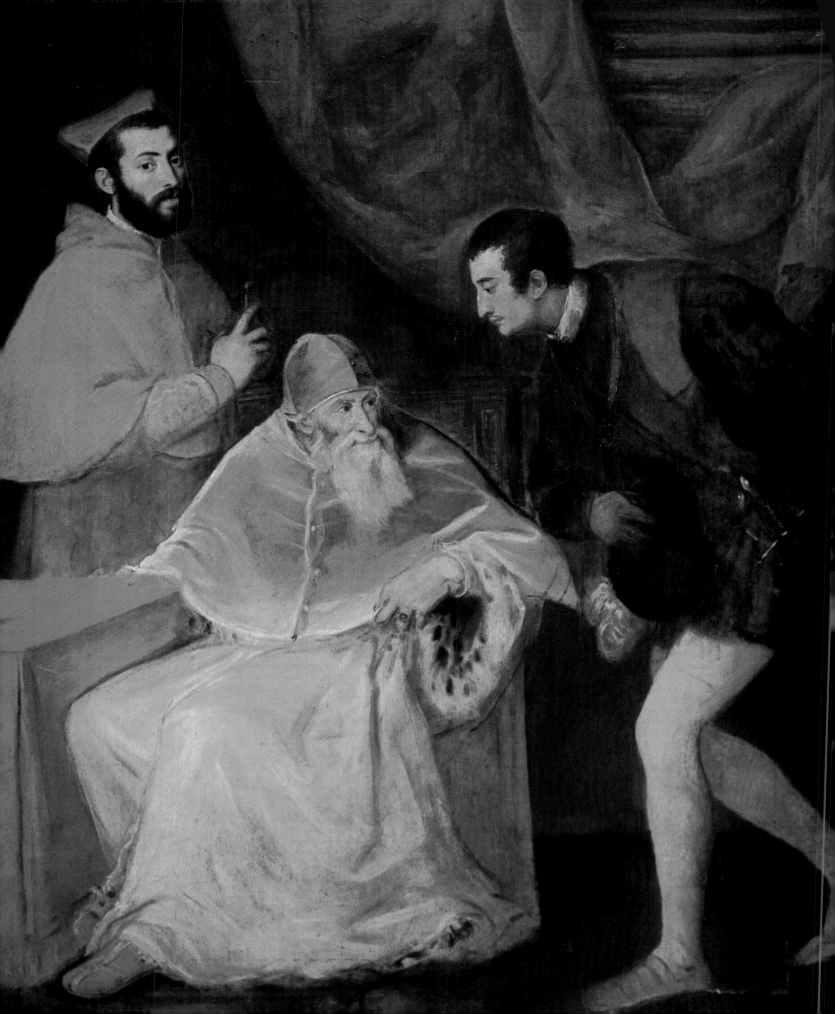

III

THE FARNESE

THE HOUSE THAT
PAUL BUILT

P ope Alexander VI Borgia had a pronounced taste for orgies, but he was also quite capable of falling in love with one woman at a time. In 1493 the woman in question was Giulia Farnese—to the great fortune of her brother Alessandro. The Farnese, a Roman family that had only recently risen above the middle class, were neither very rich nor very noble, but Alessandro was a social climber. And when the lovely Giulia one evening asked her lover to make Alessandro a cardinal, the infatuated pope could not refuse.

The Church, as everyone in high society realized, offered a career like any other, but few prelates had depended so entirely on sex for their promotion as Alessandro had, and so the twenty-five-year-old Cardinal Farnese became known as "the petticoat cardinal." The young man turned out to be one of Alexander VI's better appointments, however. Intelligent, energetic, cultivated, he also had a good nose for power. Although he owed the start of his career to a Borgia, he managed to ingratiate himself with every successive pontiff as well. In 1534, after Clement VII's death, the conclave of

Pope Paul III, born Alessandro Farnese, sits here between his grandsons Ottavio (right) and Alessandro—a cardinal—for the great portraitist Titian in 1546.

Pier Luigi, one of four children fathered by Alessandro Farnese before he became Pope Paul III, strikes a pose in Titian's portrait of 1546. Paul III's politicking won Pier Luigi several titles, the highest being duke of Parma and Piacenza.

cardinals quickly agreed on the rich, experienced, and brilliant Cardinal Farnese, who became Pope Paul III. Soon the Farnese began to feel dynastic aspirations—not a novel sensation, perhaps, except for the intensity of their desire and for their capacity to work for the same goal generation after generation.

By the time Paul III was elected, the politics of Europe and of the Church were in flux. The sack of Rome in 1527 had established the Holy Roman Emperor's superiority in Italy: Italian princes had to bow to the will of Charles V. In Germany the brilliant young theologian Martin Luther, disgusted by the corruption of the Roman clergy and by other Church practices, had challenged the spiritual authority of the Church and started the Reformation. His ideas soon spread throughout Europe and proved to be the most dangerous challenge ever faced by Rome.

The Church realized that something would have to be done to meet this challenge. In most respects, however, Paul III was a typical Renaissance pope. He loved luxury and the arts; he had children, although—unlike some of his predecessors—he never flaunted his mistresses; and he commissioned great works of art. He engaged Michelangelo to design a splendid palace for the Farnese in Rome and to paint the *Last Judgment* in the Sistine Chapel at the Vatican. Like Lorenzo, like Isabella, Paul loved pomp and ceremonies, and Rome was particularly festive under his reign.

Yet for all his love of pleasure, he was also an astute politician. Unlike Clement VII, under whose rule Rome had been sacked, he managed to stay neutral in the quarrels between France and the Hapsburgs—the ruling house of Spain and Austria. More remarkably still, in 1538 he went to Nice and there, in person, negotiated a ten-year truce between Francis I of France and Charles V, who had been at war for many years. Though he never thought of changing his own life-style, he realized that the Church must reform if it was to survive the Protestant onslaught, and he therefore admonished the cardinals to live more modestly. He apppointed commissions to investigate conditions within the Church and suggest improvements. After many efforts he summoned the Council of Trent, which met in the little north Italian town of that name and did, in fact, abolish a number of abuses. He organized the Jesuits as a semimilitary order subordinate only to the pope himself and eager to carry out his policies. He also reorganized the Inquisition—which had been set up by the Roman Catholic Church in the Middle Ages in order to fight heresy and then Protestantism—and compiled a list of forbidden books. By these and other measures, he launched the Counter-Reformation and largely set the Church pattern that prevailed for the next century.

In one respect, however, Paul III stuck firmly to the easy habits of his immediate predecessors. In 1505, while still a cardinal, he had obtained a pontifical decree legitimizing his children. Then in 1518 he arranged the marriage of his sixteen-year-old son, Pier Luigi, to Girolama Orsini, a relative of Lorenzo de' Medici's wife, and set about making sure that the young man would be treated just as well as if he belonged to one of the older Roman families.

Still, unlike them, Pier Luigi owned no land, and so he needed a career. Given the permanent state of war between France and Spain, fought out mostly on Italian soil, Pier Luigi wisely chose the military. He had received the standard classical education of the day, but he also had obvious gifts as a general. He entered the Spanish service, thus aligning himself with the more powerful side. In 1528 he won a victory against a French-led coalition and then fought in Tuscany under Ferrante Gonzaga, Isabella's son. As a reward for his success Charles V, who controlled large tracts of land throughout the peninsula, gave him an estate.

With his father's election to the papacy, Pier Luigi's career blossomed. As soon as he had the money, he began buying land in Frascati, near Rome. With a territorial base he became the equal of the other great nobles, and he went to work at once to enlarge his holdings through military conquest. In time his father appointed him gonfalonier (commander in chief) of the Church—a prestigious office that had most often gone to ruling princes in the past.

But however they might fight and connive, the Farnese still could not get hold of one of the major Italian principalities. By this time

Holding up the hands of Ottavio Farnese and Margaret of Austria, Pope Paul III celebrates the marriage he arranged to link his family with Charles V— the Holy Roman Emperor and the bride's natural father. The couple proved incompatible.

the peninsula had become, to all intents and purposes, Austro-Spanish. Its rulers owed their thrones to the goodwill of Emperor Charles V, while Milan and Naples, two of the Big Five, were outright Spanish possessions. Florence obeyed imperial orders, and Venice, weakened by Turkish attacks, found its power waning. All the way back in the 1480s, Lorenzo the Magnificent had worked hard, and successfully, to keep the foreigners out of Italy because he realized that with intervention would come subjection. The original aggressor had been France; by the 1540s the ultimate conqueror was Spain. But already, the politically and economically powerful Italy of the early Renaissance was nothing more than a faded memory.

In 1545, although Paul III knew the outlook was poor, he tried striking a great blow. The duchies of Parma and Piacenza belonged to the Church, so he simply gave them to his son in exchange for the village of Camerino, in central Italy, which was a Farnese possession. Strictly speaking this was within his power, for the duchies were subject to the pope. On the other hand, Church territory ought to have been inalienable, so that not even the supreme pontiff could give it away. Furthermore, Camerino was not a tenth of the size of Parma and Piacenza. The cardinals protested furiously. As a sop to them, the pope specified that the duchies were to be held in the sovereignty of the Church, but, in fact, he had markedly diminished the Papal States in order to secure his family's future. Isabella would have been impressed: without war Paul III had succeeded where all his predecessors had failed.

Paul intended, however, to leave more than territory to his family. He was determined also to form a huge, magnificent collection of artworks. By this time the urge to collect no longer amounted to the intellectual achievement that it had been in Medici Florence, but had instead become mere accumulation. Lorenzo and Isabella had loved objects, of course, but the splendor of their possessions had been leavened by the philosophic and artistic ferment they helped to sustain. By Paul's time the new collectors simply wanted to own more and more and more. Luckily for the Farnese, the treasures up for sale in Italy were still of very high quality. Paul III accumulated a vast

Francis I of France, astride a white horse and with Charles V on his left, enters Paris under a golden canopy in 1540. On Charles's left is Cardinal Alessandro Farnese, delegated by Pope Paul III to attend this triumphal meeting that celebrated an alliance against the Turks.

number of beautiful antique marbles in his great palaces—both the Palazzo Farnese in Rome and the Villa Farnese, which he had begun at Caprarola, outside Rome. Standing proudly on top of a hill, with a spectacular staircase marching down one side, surrounded on its other side by a vast and splendid garden, the Villa Farnese is the grandest of Roman country palaces.

For sheer magnificence, the Farnese triumphed over all their other rivals. They also outdid all rivals in purchasing a huge collection of spectacular cameos, gems, vases, sculpture, gold and silver plates and objects, tapestries, rare and costly fabrics: anything expensive. The spirit of adventurous vitality that the great Renaissance patrons had worked so hard to achieve was faded or gone.

In politics at least, Lorenzo's ideas appeared to live on. As soon as Pier Luigi took possession of his new state, he set about improving and modernizing it. He was a superb, if despotic ruler. After a careful survey of his resources, he began to improve his cities by tearing down their small, ill-kempt houses and replacing them with broader streets, and modern, light buildings. He created new jobs, improved the lot of the poor, and made it possible for the peasants to own the land they worked. Finally, he encouraged trade. And of course the local merchants appreciated the presence of a little court in Piacenza, Pier Luigi's capital. All these new policies would have been admirable had they not infringed on centuries-old feudal privileges. Since they did, the duke soon found himself with the almost unanimous opposition of his nobility.

At the same time his foreign policy was innovative—and dangerous. Although he loyally arranged to have one son, Ottavio, marry Margaret of Austria—the emperor's illegitimate daughter—he also formed an alliance with France. Another son, Orazio, married Diane of France—Henry II's illegitimate offspring. And while Orazio went off to head the imperial troops in Italy, Pier Luigi himself supported the French party in Genoa's internecine conflicts. This two-faced policy might have been sound in 1490; but in the late 1540s it was catastrophic.

Charles V, rendered anxious by Pier Luigi's divided loyalties, had

TEXT CONTINUED ON PAGE 86

Heracles rests atop Cardinal Alessandro Farnese's gilded box, a miniature but perfectly proportioned work of architecture. The stonecutter Giovanni dei Bernardi carved the rock crystal ovals in its sides with battles, revels, and other events from classical literature. Manno di Sebastiano Sbarri, a Florentine goldsmith, made the other ornaments. Heracles and the Roman gods seated at each corner show the influence of the great interpreter of human form, Michelangelo.

THE CARDINAL'S CASKET

I t was to be a "work of...perfection" expressing the "most beautiful fantasies of the Cardinal," wrote the fashionable sixteenth-century painter Giorgio Vasari of the small silver-gilt box that Cardinal Alessandro Farnese had ordered. The cardinal, grandson of Pope Paul III, was not to be disappointed. In a creation only about twenty inches high and seventeen inches wide, the designers richly demonstrated the cardinal's distinct and specific concerns.

In the sixteenth century, as the Farnese family rose to dominate Rome, two Farnese in particular changed the cultural climate and look of that city. First Pope Paul III had assigned Michelangelo, a proven genius of painting, sculpture, and architecture, to refurbish churches, palaces, and a plaza. Cardinal Alessandro followed the precedent. A scholar and sybarite with keen public-mindedness, he led Rome in a resurgence of intellectual and artistic vitality. His faith in the power of human thought, so long as it was inspired by classical Greece and Rome, shaped the cardinal's luxurious private life and his public works, such as the founding of schools of canon law, science, and theology.

The little casket, decked out like a public building and featuring learned references as well as the Farnese coat of arms, probably served the cardinal as a storage chest for some treasured manuscript. In precious metal, enamel, and gemstones, it celebrates the cardinal's civic spirit and his belief in the natural nobility of man.

The columnar figure with flexed elbows at right—a detail from the casket opposite—displays Cardinal Farnese's enameled coat of arms: blue fleurs-de-lis on a shield wreathed in the red tassels emblematic of the cardinal's office. Lapis lazuli fills the recesses.

A kissing couple, draped in the antique manner, reclines above one of the rock crystal panels. A plaque overhead bears a garbled inscription in Latin and Greek. The goldsmith seemingly lacked classical learning.

One of the four sphinxes at the base of the Farnese casket helping to support its ponderous weight, is cushioned by a sculpted cloth on her head. On her shoulders lie streamers suggesting a headdress of ancient Egypt, home of this mythical being.

TEXT CONTINUED FROM PAGE 81

other reasons to oppose the Farnese: Parma occupied a strong strategic position. If the pope gave it up, then the emperor wanted it for himself. To complicate affairs even more—and decisively—Pier Luigi had the nerve to keep for himself an imperial fief within the Parma territory that actually belonged to Ferrante Gonzaga, now governor of Milan. Under these circumstances, Pier Luigi had more enemies than he could handle.

During the summer of 1547, Ferrante came to an agreement with the nobles of the duchies who bitterly resented Pier Luigi's policy of centralization. On September 10 a group of disgruntled nobles gained entrance to the new Piacenza citadel, murdered the duke's guards, killed Pier Luigi himself, and, as a large crowd stood by and watched, flung his body into the moat. Ferrante promptly claimed and occupied Piacenza in the emperor's name. Farnese rule had ended, apparently, after a mere two years. In Rome the thunderstruck, seventy-nine-year-old Paul III, worried by all the opposition he had stirred up, simply announced that the Church was taking back the two duchies.

Luckily for the Farnese, Pier Luigi's son Ottavio was not as easily overawed as his grandfather. He had always been known as a cool, but clever and tenacious, young man. After a brief military career, during which he had led the emperor's troops against the Protestants in Germany, he had been awarded the Order of the Golden Fleece— then the most prestigious order in Europe—as well as the little duchy of Castro, vacated when his father had received Parma and Piacenza. Rushing to Parma, where his father had been very popular, he met enthusiastic crowds and took the throne as the new duke. Then, resisting his grandfather's policy, he retired to the duchy's strongest fortress—Torrechiaro—to hold out in the name of the Farnese, even against the head of the family, who also was head of the Church. To give up and return to Rome after losing the duchies would not only have been humiliating for Ottavio, but would also have made his home life intolerable: there was no prouder, or more ill-tempered, woman in Italy than his wife, Margaret.

From the very first the emperor's daughter, conveniently forget-

AN OPENING ON THE WORLD

In the Villa Farnese map room, borders of panels divide heaven (the starry ceiling) from earth (the map-covered walls).

At Caprarola, about thirty miles north of Rome, Cardinal Alessandro Farnese built the pentagonal Villa Farnese as a refuge from the intrigues of city life—a place where he might enjoy the harmonious pleasures of nature, of family, and of learning. Its windows gave a sweeping view of plain and mountain. Sunlit apartments opened onto gardens. And a sequence of staterooms culminated in the splendid map room, above and opposite.

Most educated Italians of the late sixteenth century took a keen interest in the developing earth sciences. At the cardinal's request painters masked the map room's ceiling with the signs of the zodiac and covered its walls with maps of continents, of countries, and one of the whole known world—projected with impressive accuracy. America had been discovered less than a hundred years before, and in the comfort of his villa the cardinal could track the wonderful voyage of his countryman Christopher Columbus.

On an end wall a map of the known world shows America, Asia, Africa, and Europe framed by four female figures, one for each of the continents.

ting her illegitimacy, had considered herself much too good for the little Farnese she had married. Not only was she a Hapsburg, but her first husband, Alessandro de' Medici, had been duke of Florence. Unfortunately he had also been murdered shortly after the wedding, and Margaret found herself paired with a young man whose only claim to distinction—or so she thought—was that the pope was his grandfather. Charles V, who was very fond of her, tried to placate her by giving her extensive estates of her own. But she still hated Ottavio. When they married he was not yet fourteen years old, while she herself, at sixteen, had already been married and widowed.

Had Ottavio simply given up the duchies, he could hardly have faced Margaret's ire. More than that, he knew she could be an asset, a channel through which he might convince the emperor to let him keep Parma at least. So, ignoring the fact that Charles V had conspired in Pier Luigi's murder, Ottavio enlisted the help of his older brother, the current Cardinal Alessandro Farnese, and opened negotiations with Charles V.

Alessandro Farnese's appointment to the College of Cardinals had been one of their grandfather's first acts of nepotism when he was elected pope. In the years since, the young man had become a power in Italian ecclesiastical circles and an important statesman. While Ottavio, like Pier Luigi before him, had geographically expanded Farnese interest through feats of arms, Alessandro remained in Rome, adding luster to the family name by his patronage of learning and the arts and his reputation as a collector.

Scholars from all parts of Europe visited him, advised him on the collection of books and antiquities, and joined in his intellectual projects. He grew famous as a connoisseur, selecting innumerable paintings, sculptures, decorative objects, and gemstones to be displayed in the Palazzo Farnese. Virtually all of the most accomplished artists and craftsmen of the day worked under his direction. It was he who, in time, completed the beautiful Villa Farnese at Caprarola, which Paul had begun. Alessandro was, as well, an avid womanizer—a pastime that disconcerted Pope Paul but did not lessen the confidence he placed in his second-favorite grandson.

More than five hundred ships carrying eighty thousand galley slaves, sailors, and soldiers formed the united papal, Spanish, and Venetian fleet that routed the Turks in the Gulf of Lepanto, above, in 1571. In this battle a third Alessandro Farnese, great-grandson of the pope and nephew of the cardinal, first showed the mettle for which he became famous.

In 1549 Ottavio, whom the pope loved best, remained aloof at Torrechiaro, his pathway blocked by a papal army. But he refused his grandfather's summons to come to Rome and restore family solidarity. Frustrated and mortally shocked, the aged pontiff took to his bed and grew steadily weaker. Alessandro pressed him to restore the duchies to Ottavio. In the end, reversing his policy, Paul recognized Ottavio as duke of Parma (but not Piacenza). Later on, when Paul's successor Julius III confirmed the grant, the emperor, too, bowed to Margaret's ceaseless pleas and agreed to give Parma (but not Piacenza) to Ottavio. In 1550, leaving his stronghold at last, Ottavio reentered the city he had won by dogged persistence, although not until 1552 did a treaty between France, Spain, and the pope confirm his tenure, and not until 1556 did he finally recover Piacenza.

Even then the cost was high. Not only did the duke hold his lands at the behest of Spain, but a Spanish occupation force permanently held the citadel of Piacenza. The days of independent Italian states were over now: the peninsula had become one more possession in the vast empire that stretched from South America to Sicily.

Yet the Spanish domination did help Ottavio in two respects. First, it neatly relieved him of Margaret. In 1556, after her brother Philip II succeeded Charles V as king of Spain, he appointed her governor of the Netherlands, and she went off to Brussels, thereby making her husband's life pleasanter. Even more important, with Philip's backing, Ottavio was able to pursue the modernizing, centralizing policies inaugurated by Pier Luigi. In short order he turned the once-powerful feudal lords into mere aristocrats, improved the cities, and assisted farmers and merchants. Parma became the capital of the double duchy. And the Farnese's control was confirmed when, in 1566, the duke received the title of gonfalonier from Pius V. As Italy had settled down, this great title had tended to become hereditary, so the Farnese could at last feel reasonably secure in the possession of that envied distinction.

Now and again there were rumblings. In 1578, for instance, the nobles organized yet another feudal plot against the duke, but he discovered it in time. After that, very little changed in the peaceful

The third Alessandro Farnese, also third duke of Parma, spent his youth at the court of Philip II of Spain, being tutored in fighting skills. Spanish military might and Spanish fashions, such as the ruffled collar and short beard that Alessandro wears here, dominated much of late sixteenth-century Europe.

double duchy, with only one important exception. In 1585 Philip II removed the Spanish garrison from Piacenza. Ottavio had recovered his independence.

But now another Farnese took his place at center stage, the son and heir, Alessandro. Partly as a safety measure, partly at Margaret's order, young Alessandro had been raised in Madrid. Early on he showed signs of military talent. By his early twenties he had become Philip II's most promising general and thereafter proceeded to dazzle Europe in campaign after campaign, under conditions that would have brought disaster to anyone else. Because the Spanish Netherlands had revolted against Philip, Alessandro found himself—with insufficient supplies and virtually no money—fighting the highly motivated Dutch in their homeland. In spite of this, to everyone's amazement he kept winning and soon became the terror of all Protestant powers.

He was so essential to Spain, in fact, that even when he succeeded to the duchy of Parma, in 1586, Philip II refused to let him go home to Italy. Though he was duke of Parma, he had spent his life elsewhere; he was not a familiar figure at the Farnese palaces in and near Rome either. Connected more closely with Spain and Austria than with Italy, Alessandro was a soldier. He had no time to build palaces, and his treasures were those of the battlefield and the parade ground—swords, shields, fine armor.

By this time the Counter-Reformation was in full force, and Italy was a mere agglomerate of funny little, old-fashioned states. The popes, supported by Spain and having become thoroughly alarmed by the spread of the Reformation, had embarked upon a campaign to solidify the Church. Riotous living, famous mistresses, and bastards were out of fashion. The most absolute obedience to Rome, as enforced by the Jesuits, came to be the norm; and the Vatican promulgated a new dogma. In these new, harder times the ruling houses of Italy and the Church discouraged intellectual inquiry and promoted art simply to glorify themselves. And as the Farnese consolidated their power, the world looked away from Italy, where the Renaissance had withered.

A DAMASCENED SUIT

A silvered-steel harpy (above), the mythical Greek harbinger of pain and famine, stares from the top of the third Alessandro Farnese's ceremonial armor.

The ancestral Farnese talent for warfare reached its apogee in the third Alessandro Farnese—the great-grandson of Pope Paul III—who was born in 1545. In the service of Philip II of Spain, Alessandro became a principal military commander of the age. The king presented him with this splendid armor, perhaps one of the few treasures Alessandro retained from a lifetime of triumphs.

Philip commissioned the matching ensemble for rider and horse from a master armorer of Milan, who probably took two years to complete it. But Alessandro may never have put it on. Richly ornamented with emblems of heroism and grandeur, the armor was suited to a state procession, not to the muddy battlefields where he served—first as a fiercely eager young soldier and later as governor-general of the rebellious Netherlands. While Philip's appointment of Alessandro to high command developed him as a brilliant strategist and military engineer, it left him neither taste nor leisure for pomp. Philip gave him too little money to pay his troops and no relief from the task of subduing the many Protestant factions that wanted to rid themselves of their Spanish sovereign.

When Alessandro died at forty-seven, of a wound made worse by his exhausting career, the parade armor remained shining and intact. He had stored it away when he received it and had found no use for it since.

Fitted to Alessandro Farnese, who was only about five feet tall, the suit at right has a design common to late sixteenth-century battle armor. However, its lavish decoration is exceptional and was crafted single-handedly by Lucio Piccinino, one of Milan's preeminent armorers. His techniques included damascening—the application of gold and silver to the bluesteel surface—embossing, and casting of sculptured ornaments such as the harpy on the crest of the helmet, opposite and in detail on page 91.

The high flange on the armor's left shoulder (opposite) is meant to protect the left side of the wearer's neck, a vital spot vulnerable to the attacks of right-handed swordsmen. Below the flange is a bestial face with pricked ears, perhaps a personification of foxy cunning or wolfish rapacity. Raised ornaments such as this and the numerous others here—clothlike swags, nudes, and legendary creatures—prohibited the armor's use in combat despite its utilitarian form. Combat armor required smooth plates to deflect an attacker's blows.

A model of virility—a scowling lion's head with pug nose and heavy mane—comprises the boss of an elbow guard on Alessandro's armor. When the arm is bent, the roundel attached to the lion swivels, keeping the guard positioned over the wearer's fragile elbow bones. The color of the armor's fundamental steel, visible beneath its gold and silver encrustations, was called blue and was achieved by tempering in fire. The exact heat treatment needed to create a certain color of steel was the armorer's professional secret.

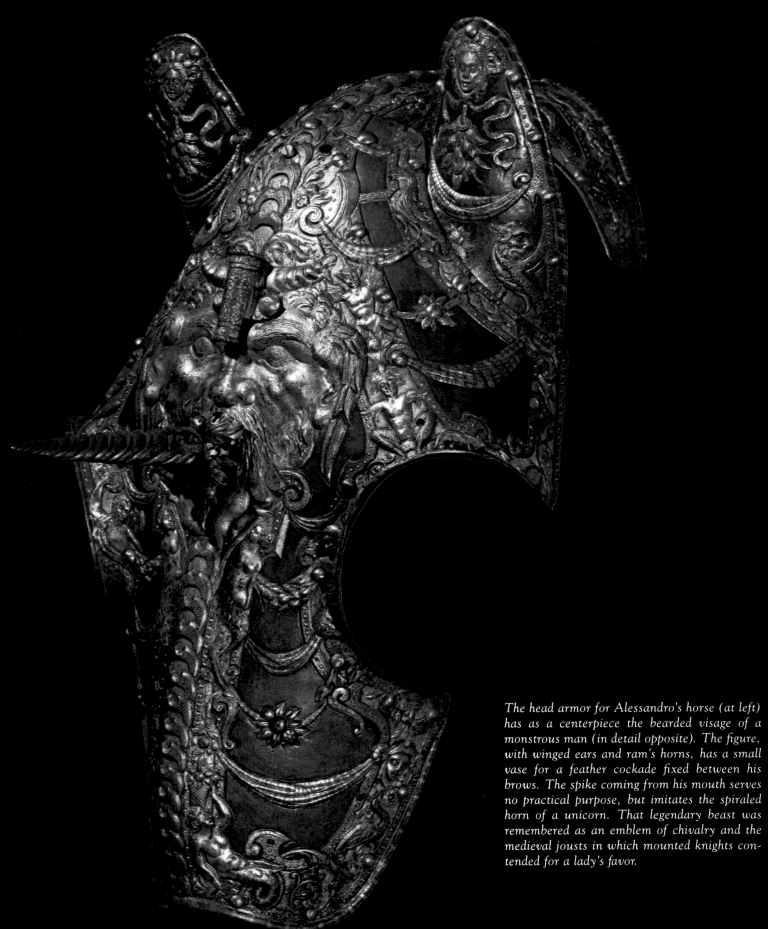

The head armor for Alessandro's horse (at left) has as a centerpiece the bearded visage of a monstrous man (in detail opposite). The figure, with winged ears and ram's horns, has a small vase for a feather cockade fixed between his brows. The spike coming from his mouth serves no practical purpose, but imitates the spiraled horn of a unicorn. That legendary beast was remembered as an emblem of chivalry and the medieval jousts in which mounted knights contended for a lady's favor.

The armor ordered by Philip II for Alessandro's mount consisted of the headpiece on page 98 and the massive steel-clad saddle above. Its wooden frame, rising high in the front and back, has a broad seat lined with quilted velvet, and its intricately embossed and damascened panels resemble those of the suit of armor it accompanied. A procession of fauns—half human and half goat—caper up each side of the saddle front to its pommel, in detail opposite. The medallion at the pommel's center displays a scene from the adventures of Heracles. With his characteristic lion skin slung across his back, he embraces a falling centaur, half man and half horse, whom he has wounded and then recognized as a long lost friend from his childhood.

OVERLEAF: On the back of the saddle shown above, fauns and gesturing women frame a scenic medallion. Inside the medallion Heracles—club raised—fights with Cerberus, the three-headed watchdog of hell, in an epic battle from Greek myth.

IV

THE ESTE OF FERRARA

"ALL FOR PLEASURE"

A few miles outside of Rome, all up and down the side of a hill, water spouts in a thousand ways from an extraordinary number of carved stone fountains. Here it jets straight up into the air; there it pours into an apparently endless stream; elsewhere it cascades down from basin to basin, comes out of the mouth of a stone figure, or spreads before a trompe l'oeil view of ancient Rome. Separating all these fountains are steps, terraces, and rows of tall cypresses. This pleasure garden, the most splendid in Europe, is that of the Villa d'Este—a majestic Renaissance palace in Tivoli. The Villa d'Este was conceived late in the career of Ippolito d'Este, a very wealthy cardinal who had never believed that being an ecclesiastic should in any way prevent him from enjoying the many pleasures of this world.

"The rich and merry Ippolito," as he was called, simply continued a family tradition: his parents were Alfonso d'Este, duke of Ferrara, and the notorious Lucrezia Borgia. His aunt was Isabella d'Este, and his parents' court, in fact, closely resembled Isabella's own. Like his

A gentleman-soldier who cast his own bronze weapons, Duke Alfonso I d'Este made Ferrara one of Italy's most powerful duchies in the sixteenth century.

Lucrezia Borgia, above, daughter of Pope Alexander VI, married Alfonso in a dazzling wedding ceremony in 1502. Bored with Alfonso, the duchess apparently returned the affections of many who found her beautiful and intelligent: her flirtations scandalized Ferrara and embarrassed her husband.

sister, Alfonso spent his life trying to align himself with whoever was the leading power, so his switches were numerous, confusing, and sometimes dangerous. At one point he was excommunicated and almost lost his estates, but he managed to be received back into the Church while actually extending his territory. At the same time he ruled over a highly literate court—Ariosto, Isabella's favorite poet, was long its finest ornament. And Lucrezia Borgia, his wife, apparently anxious to bury her lurid past, turned into a well-behaved, charming sovereign who patronized the arts. That she also had a long affair with Cardinal Pietro Bembo, a renowned scholar and hedonist, only seemed to add to her reputation for discernment and generosity. Thus Ippolito grew up in a typical Italian court—brilliant, worldly, intellectual, and dissolute.

Since he was a second son, his parents settled his fate at the time of his birth in 1509: this grandson of Pope Alexander VI would enter the Church, become a cardinal, and perhaps—with a little luck and a lot of good management—even be elected supreme pontiff. His father wasted no time in advancing Ippolito's career: in May 1519, at the age of ten, Ippolito became a priest. Soon after, he became a bishop so that his uncle, another Ippolito, could pass the archdiocese of Milan on to him. Boys of ten seldom rose to be bishops, even in Renaissance Italy, but Ippolito belonged to a ruling family, and no one in Milan objected. Actually, as far as Ippolito himself was concerned, being archbishop hardly made any difference in his life. He continued his education—studying Latin, Greek, philosophy, and Italian literature—and he learned how to ride, hunt, shoot, and fence just like any other upper-class boy. Then when he reached his middle teens he went to the University of Padua, where a course in theology complemented his otherwise secular studies.

Unlike some of his colleagues, Ippolito always managed to live a decorous life. He liked women and would not have dreamed of remaining chaste, but he was discreet about his sex life—so much so, in fact, that no one ever knew who his mistresses were. When in later life he suddenly introduced his full-grown daughter, no one could guess the mother's identity. But very early on he demonstrated the family taste for splendor. As archbishop of Milan he had his own, abundant income, which he spent in ways his aunt and mother must have approved.

As a result, by the time he was twenty, Ippolito owned a luxurious palace of his own in Ferrara, and when his brother Ercole married a French princess, he was able to give a spectacular ballet followed by a variety of the best entertainment. Soon, in fact, he acquired the reputation of being a man who thoroughly enjoyed the good life: his palace, his gardens, his furniture, his jewels—all were rich and elegant. But along with his taste for luxury went a searching, informed intelligence. Ippolito's library was quite as splendid as his silver; his taste for lively conversation, fine painting, and good poetry always remained essential to his character.

A well-to-do young man in those days needed to understand politics. All through the 1520s and 1530s Ippolito was a participant in his father's often dangerous decisions and was able to see at first hand just how difficult survival could be. By 1530 the duke had annexed the nearby duchy of Modena, thus almost doubling the extent of his territory; but even then his situation remained precarious. The very uncertainty of his father's position provided Ippolito with the best possible school for a future diplomat.

Ippolito's advancement was also a major preoccupation for the duke, who was anxious to have him made a cardinal so that the boy could give him a helping hand in Rome. One pope after another, however, managed to defer the coveted promotion: they, too, were aware that they might be uncomfortable having young Este looking over their shoulders. Then, in March 1536, Ercole, who needed French support, decided to send Ippolito off to France as his ambassador; the move proved to be a brilliant one.

Not only did Ippolito display an inborn flair for diplomacy, but he also felt thoroughly at home in the splendid court of Francis I. A great Renaissance figure, tall, athletic, handsome, the king loved all the pleasures—women, food, books, pageantry, and war. Like his predecessors Charles VIII and Louis XII, Francis was fascinated by Italy, its architecture, its art, and its culture. He took Leonardo da

Ippolito d'Este, framed in the seventeenth-century engraving above, won fame as a generous supporter of artists and musicians. As cardinal of Ferrara, this son of Alfonso and Lucrezia Borgia was one of the wealthiest men of the Church.

Renaissance court ladies meet at an outdoor loom, each to take her turn weaving or, with the trio in the foreground, embroidering. This scene, and the ones opposite and on pages 116–117, are from the murals at the Palazzo di Schifanoia—the Este's favorite pleasure resort in Ferrara.

Vinci into his service, provided him with a house and garden near Amboise, on the Loire river, and bought all the paintings he could. He also commissioned spectacular pieces of gold- and enamelwork from Benvenuto Cellini, the greatest goldsmith who ever lived. The court was both splendid and lively—the perfect place, in fact, for a hedonistic Italian bishop.

Although Ippolito knew the art of flattery, he quickly found that he hardly needed to use it since he shared so many of Francis's tastes. In no time at all the two became friends. Better still, the wily Italian was able to join the little circle around the king's mistress, the duchess of Etampes. He received gifts from Francis, of course—small ones, such as cups or expensive cloth, and bigger ones, such as abbeys, convents frequently blessed with large incomes. The king customarily gave one or more abbeys to his favorites; assuming the title of abbot, they kept the revenues and appointed some lowly, ill-paid cleric to discharge the absent abbot's duties.

Such practices did not do much for the reputations of churchmen. Monks and abbots were rapidly becoming symbols of greed and lechery and, in the process, fueling the fires of the early Reformation. But the custom was a great convenience for the king, who could reward his friends at no cost to himself. Within a very few years, Ippolito thus found himself enjoying the revenues of numerous French abbeys, while remaining archbishop of Milan at the same time. The Venetian ambassador reported that Ippolito was one of the richest princes of his era.

Even so, money was not enough: Ippolito still craved the cardinalate. Ever obliging, Francis I wrote the pope requesting that his protégé be nominated. Paul III balked, especially since the French ambassador to the Vatican went around reminding people that Lucrezia Borgia had led a rather checkered life and that, in this case, the sins of the mother should positively be visited upon the son. Then, in 1538, Paul III came to Nice to try to negotiate a peace between Charles V and Francis I, who had been at war, on and off, for some twenty years. Naturally Ippolito was there, and, no doubt eloquently, he pleaded for his promotion. Still, the pope delayed;

but when a few days later Charles V, who had been successfully lobbied by the wily Ippolito, asked Paul to raise the archbishop of Milan to the Sacred College, he finally gave in. On March 5, 1539, Ippolito was officially, and to his boundless joy, made a cardinal. Once this goal had been gained, there was no end to the additional honors that would be granted to the new cardinal of Ferrara.

The new cardinal's diplomatic talents were by this time so widely recognized that when Francis decided to seek an anti-Spanish alliance with the pope and Venice, he sent off Ippolito as his representative. Venice declined to join the French, but this was no reflection on the ambassador's talents. In fact one of the city's envoys soon wrote that "Cardinal d'Este is esteemed the wisest and most experienced of all the cardinals; he is endowed with a patience so incredible in all things that his like is unknown." As soon as France and Spain finally made peace, Ippolito set off for France and found himself more in favor than ever. Glorying in his position at court, he hired the king's Italian architect and built himself a sumptuous villa near the palace of Fontainebleau, about thirty-five miles southeast of Paris—then Francis's favorite residence.

The king's death, in March 1547, was a blow. The new king, Henry II, had his own mistress and his own friends. The cardinal did give him the grandest of receptions in Lyon, of which he was now archbishop, but it seemed likely that the great days of his favor had vanished. But then, to most people's surprise, Henry II, a dull, dour, and obstinate monarch, realized that Ippolito was a great asset, and he continued his father's support. He realized, too, that if he used his influence to have Ippolito elected pope, France would be strengthened in its rivalry with Charles V. In 1549, therefore, when the aged Paul III finally died, the cardinal of Ferrara went off to the conclave with Henry's full backing.

The emperor knew of all this scheming, however. At conclave after conclave he interposed his veto: in 1550, when Julius III was elected; in 1555, when he was replaced by Marcellus II; again in 1555, when it was Paul IV's turn; in 1559, when Pius IV won; and finally in 1566, when Pius V became pontiff. At all five of these

TEXT CONTINUED ON PAGE 116

Amorous, golden-haired courtiers enjoy a spring day in a scene inspired by the romantic life of those in Italy's princely circles. Some of the ladies in the group hold mandolins and flutes.

A LITTLE
NIGHT MUSIC

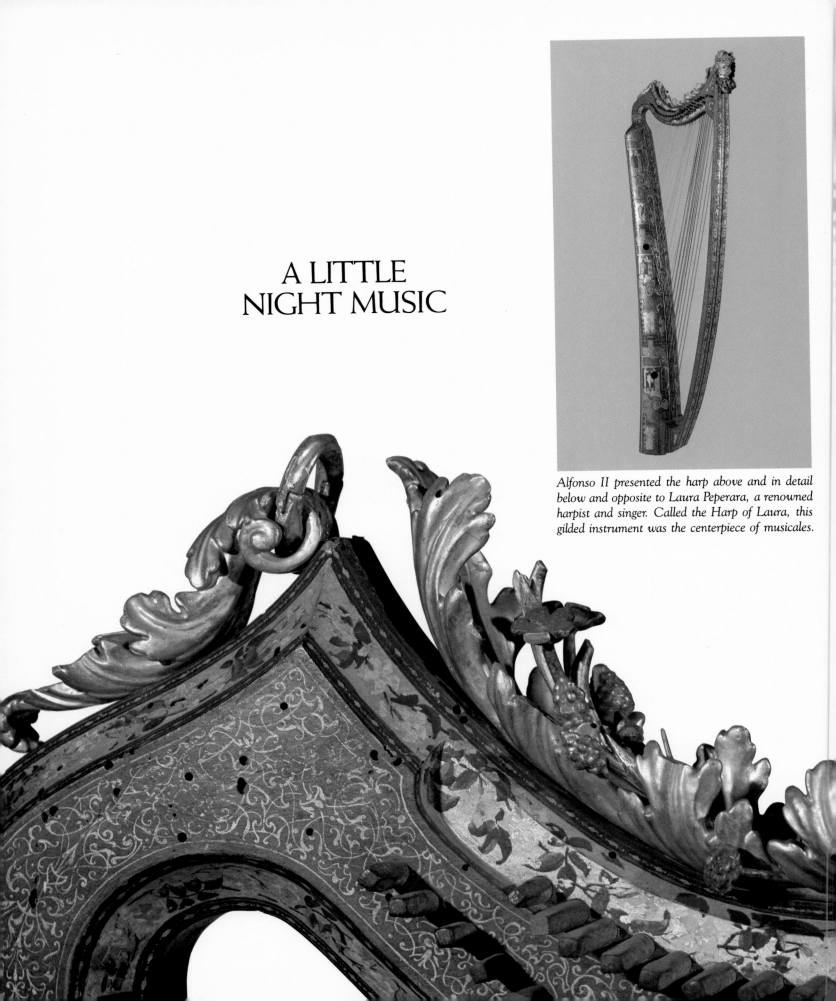

Alfonso II presented the harp above and in detail below and opposite to Laura Peperara, a renowned harpist and singer. Called the Harp of Laura, this gilded instrument was the centerpiece of musicales.

Music, so long confined to the Church, became part of secular life in sixteenth-century Italy. Musicians and singers filled Italy's princely courts with joyous sounds: the perfect accompaniment to the intellectual, artistic, and philosophical pursuits of the Renaissance courts. The Este family surrounded themselves with instrumentalists, composers, and singers of their duchy, making Ferrara one of Europe's major music centers. Alfonso II—grandson of Alfonso I—set the tone by holding nightly concerts in his palace and hiring musicians to play at banquets, picnics, and poetry readings. The Este and other wealthy music lovers amassed great collections of instruments, three elegant examples of which are on these pages.

The instruments, fashioned from the finest woods and decorated with classical motifs, were masterpieces, even when mute. Though the Este hired performers, ladies and gentlemen of the time were expected not only to appreciate music, but also to make it: to complete the mastery of social graces, a duke or duchess had to know how to blow a horn or strum a guitar.

In a society that valued music so highly, the acquisition of instruments and of performers to play them became competitive, and courts vied for virtuosos. But for all the pleasure it gave, music was more than mere entertainment to the Este. Like the ancient Greeks they so idealized, the men and women of Renaissance Italy believed that music possessed magical powers to stir the soul.

Ferrara artist Giulio Marescotti decorated the Harp of Laura with golden arabesques and floral shapes such as those in the detail above. Forty-nine strings attach to the wooden harp.

A sensuous sculpture as well as a musical instrument, the seven-stringed lira above (front and back) is carved with male and female faces and torsos. The tiny ivory plaque set into the back of the instrument, in detail opposite, bears a Greek inscription that was a Renaissance credo: "Music is the solace of mankind."

Ebony and ivory stripe the body of this pandurina, a slender, sixteenth-century curiosity that makers of musical instruments developed from the more popular, and chubbier, mandolin. A player, privileged to entertain at a banquet or other exclusive court gathering, plucked the pandurina's four strings—usually to accompany a woman's voice.

TEXT CONTINUED FROM PAGE 109

elections, in spite of the best efforts France and Ferrara could muster, Ippolito failed to get the majority of the votes he needed to emerge as the supreme pontiff. He came to realize that he would fail in his greatest ambition, not just because of the emperor's opposition, but also because his fellow cardinals found him more and more at odds with the spirit of the times.

By the 1550s the Counter-Reformation was in full swing. Not only did the popes enforce new, stricter dogma, but the faithful had come to expect churchmen to behave as if they really were men of God. Bishops, for instance, tended the spiritual and physical needs of their flocks, led relatively austere lives, and set a moral example. Ippolito, unfortunately and conspicuously, stood for the exact opposite of all such rigorous behavior. Besides leading a spectacularly luxurious life, he had accumulated all those abbeys and bishoprics—more than he could possibly administer—and he scarcely visited any of them. Ippolito was carrying on the best Renaissance tradition, and his fellow churchmen alternated between embarrassment and anger whenever his name came up. "The Cardinal of Ferrara is a very splendid and most noble lord," the Florentine ambassador reported, "and for family, richness and following there is perhaps no one his equal in this Sacred College. However there are not lacking those who accuse him of wishing to show too much pride." He refused to change, to adapt to the new mood, and his many palaces filled with treasures all worked against him.

Although Ippolito could never become pope himself, he was again and again able to push the candidate of his choice to victory. In 1550 he boosted the candidacy of the austere cardinal del Monte, who was not only properly anti-Protestant, but also knew how to listen to the advice of his betters. As Julius III, del Monte immediately manifested his gratitude by making Ippolito governor of Tivoli. The governorship was a great honor, and when Ippolito went to take up his post, one hundred gentlemen met him four miles from the city and escorted him to Tivoli's gate. There, to the cannon's thunder, a hundred boys bearing palms received him and led him to a triumphal arch. In front of the arch, a citizen dressed to look like the emperor

Workers in belted tunics prune grape vines in an Este vineyard. By cutting back the vines in March, grape growers could postpone the growth of fragile new leaves and buds, lessening the danger of late spring frosts. Prominent families such as the Este cultivated their own vineyards and enjoyed the prestige of having a personal vintage.

Titus, who had supposedly founded Tivoli in the first century A.D., recited a speech in praise of the new governor. The bishop and the chief magistrate then welcomed Ippolito, and he rode the rest of the way to his official residence in a triumphal chariot drawn by what one viewer called "Moorish slaves." And then Ippolito discovered that his new home was nothing more than a dank, dark old convent—a residence that obviously would not do.

The cardinal started at once to plan a new home, the Villa d'Este. Its construction involved an enormous amount of work and expenditure. Set high on top of a hill, the grand palace—fitted out with loggia, terraces, and frescoes—dominated the landscape. Behind the palace, gardens covered the entire steep slope; and since the architect, Pirro Ligorio, had suggested a great many fountains, miles of pipes had to be laid. The final effect was stunning and immediately famous throughout Europe. But it was certainly a provocative display of incurable worldliness, and it did much to injure the cardinal's already tattered reputation. His most splendid possession may well have been his greatest encumbrance.

Luckily the popes remembered that Ippolito was also a top diplomat. He was involved in all the negotiations that followed the constant wars taking place in northern Italy. He represented the French king, for instance, as well as the pope, when the status of Parma was settled in Ottavio Farnese's favor. For a while the pontiff appointed him governor of Siena, which then reverted to Florence; all through the 1560s Ippolito continued to function at the highest level of affairs. Even the popes who did not like him realized he was too clever to waste. Now and again, however, pontifical hatred won the day. Some of the popes resented being helped, especially by a man who felt himself their superior. During the brief pontificate of Paul IV, Ippolito was forced to retire to France.

From time to time a pope would call him out of retirement, but the Church realized that Ippolito belonged to an earlier, more tolerant time. His collection of bishoprics and abbeys seemed more scandalous year by year. But when anyone suggested that the cardinal divest himself of all but one—and then take up residence as a proper clergyman—he refused to take such a notion at all seriously.

Aside from all other considerations, he had too many palaces to choose from. In addition to his palaces at Fontainebleau and Ferrara, he owned a sumptuous villa at Belfiore just outside the city. In Rome he had his town palace, as well as his villa on the hill of Montecavallo, with its magnificent gardens in which he had installed statues of Roman gods and goddesses—classical subjects that hardly looked appropriate in the new and ultrareligious atmosphere. Besides these, Ippolito had the villa in Tivoli.

Like a true Renaissance man, Ippolito insisted on surrounding himself with beauty. He bought ceaselessly from Cellini, and his gold table service became famous. He collected antique statuary, paintings, medals, bronzes. He surrounded himself with a court of artists and writers, men such as Torquato Tasso, unquestionably one of the greatest Italian poets; Giovanni Palestrina, the century's greatest composer; and the painters Palma the Younger, Sebastiano del Piombo, and Federigo Zuccaro. He owned a vast library and had his own mosaicists, sculptors, engravers, tapestry weavers, and majolica makers. Finally, in the villa and gardens at Tivoli, he brought to its apotheosis the Renaissance feeling for openness and nature, tamed and made more glorious, which had first appeared in the Medici villas outside Florence. Unlike the small, enclosed medieval gardens, the park represented that thirst for pleasure so characteristic of the Renaissance. Hills, fountains, vistas—all were used to create outdoors the same kind of expansive beauty to be seen in the works of Botticelli. At the Villa d'Este, Ippolito created the best, the most beautiful of the gardens of the Renaissance.

Of course it was all for pleasure. As the Counter-Reformation grew progressively stronger, people thought the Church should be spending its money in more serious ways. A spectacular garden, created solely because its owner loved beautiful things, may have been typical of all the Renaissance stood for, but by 1570 a cardinal of the Church could no longer indulge in this kind of display without severe criticism. Ippolito, in fact, had outlived his times. In doing so, he managed to give the sunset of the age a lasting, effulgent glory.

THE DELIGHTS OF WATER

A broad walk leads to the Fountain of the Dragon, one of the magnificent water displays on the grounds of the Villa d'Este, which rises in the background.

On September 9, 1550, Cardinal Ippolito d'Este arrived in the town of Tivoli, twenty miles east of Rome, where he was tumultuously welcomed as the new governor. Tivoli and its territories had long been a favorite country retreat for wealthy Romans, and the governorship was a consolation prize for the forty-one-year-old cardinal. Possibly the most adroit diplomat in the Church, Ippolito nevertheless failed to achieve his dream of becoming pope. But he had been instrumental in the choice of others, and after the 1550 conclave that elected Julius III, the grateful pontiff appointed Ippolito governor of Tivoli for life.

Accustomed to splendid surroundings, the cardinal found his official residence in Tivoli disappointing and decided to transform the broken-down old monastery into a villa—the luxurious country house identified with upper-class living in Italy. Not surprisingly the inspiration for Renaissance villas came from the ancient Romans, who built them both as retreats from urban life and to show off their wealth more expansively than was possible in the city. Indeed the hills around Tivoli still held the ruins of villas once inhabited by illustrious generals and emperors; and Ippolito commissioned Pirro Ligorio, his personal architect and antiquarian, to excavate a number of them. The erudite Ligorio not only drew upon these ruins in planning the enormous Villa d'Este, but he also unearthed a priceless trove of antique statues that, placed on display, became one of the villa's outstanding features.

Its most remarkable feature, however, was the dramatic use of water within the garden. Meticulously laid out by Ligorio, the garden extended over two steep slopes, descending in tiers like an amphitheater to a broad terrace. To furnish the garden with water, engineers between 1561 and 1564 constructed two great aqueducts, one of which tapped the powerful Aniene River that flows into the Tiber just above Rome. Then, over the next seven years, artisans created a series of waterworks—fountains, pools, grottoes—along the major walks and intersecting pathways.

For Ippolito and his guests, a stroll through the garden offered delights of sight, sound, and touch. Ligorio exploited the fluidity of water, not just its movement, so that the water had a sculptural quality. High piercing jets vied with deafening cascades or with water gurgling down steps and channels. Turning a corner, surprised visitors might be squirted by trick fountains. And many of the major works, like those on the following pages, assumed forms that satisfied Ippolito's zest for the antique. Playful yet classical, this water architecture was a most eloquent status symbol for the last of the great Renaissance clerics.

A grotesque face stares out from one end of the Path of the Hundred Fountains. After walking alongside its numerous spouts (in greater detail on pages 128–129), a stroller could ascend the stairs here and continue on to the villa's principal waterfall, the Oval Fountain, visible in the background.

OVERLEAF: *In this view of the Oval Fountain, a great veil of water flows from a basin into a huge pool, whose elliptical shape gave the fountain its name. In back of the fountain is a leafy arcade with a series of archways and a walkway along the top, displaying Roman-inspired statues (in detail on pages 124–127). In front of the cascade is a winged figure emerging from a seashell.*

Among the works recreating antique forms is the sculpture opposite of a seated woman resting her right arm on the back of a nude boy. She represents one of the prophetesses from Greco-Roman mythology known as sibyls—in this instance the sibyl Albunea, whom the ancient Romans associated with the Tivoli region. The curly headed child in detail at right is probably the son of a sea nymph linked in legend with Albunea. Designed by the cardinal's architect Pirro Ligorio, and handsomely carved from the local limestone called travertine, the pair occupy a niche in rocks overlooking the Oval Fountain.

Holding a cornucopia of fruit, the bearded figure of the river god Aniene reclines in a grotto above the Oval Fountain. This

statue is one of three that Ippolito commissioned around the fountain to symbolize the three rivers flowing through Tivoli.

Jets of water gush in perfect symmetry along the Path of the Hundred Fountains, the garden's most delightful promenade. Fed by three terraced canals, the fountains actually number ninety-one and are cast in four shapes: boats, obelisks, fleurs-de-lis, and eagles (visible along the upper row). The latter two were devices of the Este family. One of the retaining walls also originally bore stucco reliefs of scenes from the Metamorphoses, a compendium of myths by the Roman poet Ovid that provided much of the artists' subject matter throughout the garden.

129

For Renaissance gentlemen and ladies, this many-breasted figure of the goddess Diana was a symbol of virtue. In Ippolito's day the statue fronted one of the garden's most unusual structures—a fountain that housed an organ played entirely by water. Rushing water drove air through the instrument's pipes, while another water-driven device moved the keys.

OVERLEAF: A flight of steps and a balustrade with spurting vases wind around the Fountain of the Dragon, which has a basin containing four giant dragons' heads (of which only three are visible here) carved from stone. The heads represent four of the one hundred heads of Ladonis—a monster from classical myth slain by Heracles—to whom Ippolito dedicated his garden. Several sixteenth-century chronicles reported, fancifully, that the cardinal had ordered that this fountain be constructed overnight in honor of a visit by Pope Gregory XIII, whose family's coat of arms bore a dragon.

Suffused with sunlight, a fierce spray bursts from one of the great heads in the Fountain of the Dragon. Partly visible on the left is an even more powerful geyser that rises in the middle of the fountain. This central jet could be varied so that it shot off explosively like gunfire—or fanned out to simulate a gentle downpour of rain.

V

THE GRAND DUKES

THE LATER MEDICI

Late at the night on January 5, 1537, Alessandro de' Medici, duke of Florence, was asleep in his palace. He had been expecting a woman; instead, his cousin Lorenzino de' Medici walked in with a hired assassin and, without a moment's hesitation, thrust his sword deep into the duke's back. There was a struggle, but finally the assassin plunged a dagger into the duke's throat. Within seconds Alessandro was dead. The murder did neither Florence nor Lorenzino much good. By disposing of the duke, his cousin had thought he would bring back the republic as it had existed after Lorenzo the Magnificent's death and, with it, the great days of the city; in fact he actually opened the way for its long slide into political mediocrity.

The leading citizens of Florence turned not to Lorenzino to lead them, but to yet another Medici: Cosimo I, known as Cosimo the Great, the head of a younger branch of the family. As for the republic that Lorenzino had hoped to restore, no one within the city had any hope for it. The republic had been reestablished in 1494 after the

Francesco de' Medici, opposite, a melancholy alchemist and a distant cousin of Lorenzo the Magnificent, ruled Florence after Lorenzo's successors lost power.

Three figures personifying strength, prudence, and silence attend Francesco's father, Cosimo, as he studies plans for an armed attack on the republic of Siena. Though disinclined to the military life, by 1570 Cosimo had subjugated all the region of Tuscany, including Siena and Florence, and had become its first grand duke.

expulsion of Piero de' Medici, but had failed—poverty and strife replacing the peace and plenty of Lorenzo's reign. Then, in 1512, when Pope Clement VII (the illegitimate son of Lorenzo's brother Giuliano) had dispatched his troops to restore the Medici to Florence, they had easily routed the republicans. In 1537, after Alessandro's murder, the republicans had no means of reviving their cause.

As it turned out, the eighteen-year-old Cosimo was the best possible choice as the new ruler. Although Florence was still, in theory, a semi-independent state, in fact it had become a direct vassal of the Hapsburgs; since the Medici were now properly obedient, Emperor Charles V simply exerted his control through them. Young Cosimo, granted the title of duke in 1537, understood all this. And while he was intent on regaining the largest possible measure of autonomy, he knew it would take time and great subtlety if ever he was to achieve his goal, which was to rule an independent, newly powerful Florence.

All through Alessandro's reign many republicans had been sent into exile; upon his death they tried to take advantage of Cosimo's youth and inexperience. They assembled an army and marched on Florence—fully expecting that the city would rise against the young tyrant—but most of the republicans had already left. Then, within days, Cosimo crushed his opponents at the battle of Prato, not far from the city walls. He followed up his victory by executing sixteen republican leaders and confiscating their estates while at the same time exiling the few people who had displayed anti-Medici feelings. By this time the Florentines knew how to take a hint. After Cosimo let people know that he was sending out hired assassins to dispose of his exiled enemies, obedience became everyone's motto.

For the next ten years, the duke set about thoroughly securing his government. In 1513, a quarter of a century earlier, Niccolò Machiavelli, a pro-Medici Florentine who worked for the city government, had written a treatise entitled *The Prince*. In this work he set forth the principles by which a state must be governed if it was to prosper. The ruler, he said, must be ruthless, secretive, and opportunistic—seizing every chance he could to create his own luck. He could do so only as long as he renounced pity, kindness, or gratitude to individuals who, in any event, would prosper in a strong, well-ordered state. People who had read Machiavelli might well have seen the duke as the incarnation of Machiavelli's guiding principles. Cosimo was unscrupulous, pitiless, and highly effective; he trusted no one. Soon after his accession he moved from the Medici palace, which was open and accessible, to the Palazzo Vecchio, the fortresslike center of the city government in Florence. Expelling the city judges from their place in the neighboring open loggia, he stationed his armed guards there instead.

As his wife he chose Eleonora of Toledo, the daughter of the Spanish viceroy of Naples, who was extremely rich. Her dowry vastly enlarged Cosimo's own fortune. She was a beautiful and arrogant aristocrat, but Cosimo got on well with her. They had eleven children—two of the sons died young, as did two of the daughters. But Cosimo's succession was secure.

As Machiavelli would have expected, Cosimo's shrewdness paid off. In 1542 war broke out again between France and Spain. As usual, Charles V needed money, so Cosimo offered a huge loan and in exchange received several additions to his territory. Even more to his benefit, he had now become the emperor's mainstay in Italy and could expect more favors. Then, in 1548, Siena revolted against its imperial master, driving out the Spanish garrison.

Cleverly, Cosimo convinced the emperor to restore the city's ancient republic and the Sienese to accept a garrison. As he almost surely expected, the compromise did not work, but he had demonstrated his own good faith to all parties. In 1552 the Sienese rose again and asked Henry II for a French garrison. In great alarm Charles V turned to Cosimo, provided him with an army, and asked him to suppress the rebellion.

The result was a long, drawn-out siege of the city. It ended only after Siena's original population, which numbered forty thousand, had shrunk to six thousand, depleted by starvation and disease. Now Cosimo got just what he wanted. Siena's spirit was broken forever, and the city was joined with Florence. At the treaty of Cateau-

On the outskirts of Florence, the Palazzo Pitti and its vast park, above, had a countrified air that appealed to Cosimo's wife, Eleonora of Toledo, whose health was frail. She bought the palace from the merchant family Pitti, moved there with her family from the inner city, and designed a garden for the park, where her younger children probably played while Francesco, her oldest son, studied government.

Eleonora proved an affectionate mother to the children she bore to Cosimo, called Cosimo the Great. While Francesco succeeded his father as grand duke, the cherubic Giovanni—here at Eleonora's side—may have been the couple's favorite.

Cambresis, which ended the final war between Charles and the French kings in 1559, both France and Spain recognized Cosimo as the ruler of all Tuscany.

He worked hard, too, to make Tuscany prosperous. By the 1560s, after some twenty peaceful years, agriculture and trade were flourishing once more. Industry had revived. Cosimo helped restore the University of Pisa, which had been sinking steadily since Lorenzo's death, and reorganized the system of public records so that the information would be more accessible. He hired good engineers and competent administrators. He rebuilt towns, reformed antiquated laws, and maintained order. Economically Tuscany had become a medium-size power. Then Cosimo made his final move. As a mere duke, by law he remained the emperor's vassal; as a grand duke he would become a fully independent sovereign on a par with other European monarchs.

Only two men could create a grand duke: the emperor and the pope. The emperor would not, so Cosimo set off on prolonged maneuvers with Rome. In the late 1560s the pope was Pius V, who believed that military force was the only way of ending the Reformation. To please him Cosimo enforced the strictest orthodoxy within his dominions. When one of the Medici family's faithful servants— who also happened to be in the service of the pope—converted to Protestantism, for example, Cosimo turned the unfortunate old man over to the authorities in Rome, and they duly burned him at the stake. Cosimo then pressed on with his campaign to be made grand duke. Meanwhile the Netherlands had risen against the Hapsburgs, and so, with the major powers too distracted to object, the pope crowned Cosimo as grand duke of Tuscany. England and France (whose regent at the time was Queen Caterina de' Medici—great-granddaughter of Lorenzo the Magnificent) immediately recognized this new European power. Within the constraints of Spanish power, the first Medici grand duke had gone as far as possible toward making Florence, once more, a respectable state.

Cosimo's interests were limited to politics. He encouraged the arts only inasmuch as they seemed to provide useful propaganda. In

1550, for instance, at Eleonora's urging he started work on the abandoned foundations of the Palazzo Pitti, high on a hill across the Arno in Florence. There, in the Boboli gardens, Cosimo's designs introduced a new notion of landscape architecture that relied often on the grotesque or the startling, especially in the grotto, where full-relief sculptures emerged from the walls. He commissioned Agnolo Bronzino, a great master, to paint portraits of his entire family. Yet in all of these commissions, he cared more for the prestige the works brought to him than for the art itself.

Four years after Cosimo received his exalted new title, he died and left his son Francesco to rule the grand duchy. Under Francesco, Tuscany inexorably slid back into its true position—that of a fifth-rate power wholly dependent on the Hapsburgs. While Florence declined, Francesco amused himself in his laboratory. At first, like many of his contemporaries, he tried to discover the so-called philosopher's stone, that mythical substance capable of turning lead into gold; but eventually he found that he was also interested in more mundane experiments. He worked out a new, improved way of making ceramics. He developed his talent for setting gems, and while he was at it, started making costume jewelry, a craft forgotten since the fall of the Roman Empire. He also excelled at smelting and glassmaking and carving crystal. He experimented with fireworks. All in all he was competent at a variety of handicrafts. The public, however, believed all along that he was concocting poisons.

Francesco was not entirely devoid of artistic feeling. He created the Uffizi Gallery, thus making the spectacular Medici collection of paintings accessible to the public. He also continued his father's tradition of patronage. He did not have the instincts of a great patron, however. When he set up free studios in the Uffizi for young painters, he did so less because he cared for young talent than because his act befitted a munificent patron. In his one great literary endeavor, he endowed the Accademia della Crusca—"Academy of the Chaff"—a body of scholars who set out in 1582 to define and refine the Italian language. Francesco was long dead when the Accademia finally published its dictionary in 1612. The work was

TEXT CONTINUED ON PAGE 146

This portrait of Bianca Capello—the longtime mistress of Francesco de' Medici and then his second wife—is one of the few that Francesco's family did not destroy in an effort to blot out Bianca's memory after her death. All Florence resented the beautiful Venetian, who was rumored to be a witch.

A PRIVATE COSMOS

When Francesco de' Medici visited the room he called his studiolo, he entered a sacred precinct in the heart of the Palazzo Vecchio—the old ducal palace from which he ineptly governed Florence. Up a secret staircase from the palace's private apartments, the studiolo was long, narrow, and windowless like an outsize strongbox. Once inside, Francesco stood at the center of a painted model of the cosmos that accorded with his pet ideas and emphasized his preoccupations: alchemy, metallurgy, mineralogy, and the decorative arts. Ceiling pictures represented the four elements of the universe—earth, air, fire, and water—as well as the earth's mineral riches, while the walls at each end showed the four seasons of the year. More than a score of talented painters from Tuscany and Flanders had lined other walls with panels illustrating the laws of nature and the human artistry these laws gave rise to. The lower panels concealed a row of cupboards, in which Francesco stored dazzling examples of such artistry: precious books, vases, sculptures, and jewels that he studied worshipfully by candlelight.

Unlike his father, Cosimo—a boldly decisive manager of the Medici domain—Francesco shrank from public life. He compared himself to Solomon—the biblical king whose arcane knowledge alchemists revered—and wished to command the mysteries of the universe rather than the affairs of his hometown. Closed in his studiolo he could flatter himself that he did so.

In the oblong studiolo, right, in the lunette at the top of its far wall, a round portrait of Francesco's mother, Eleonora, symbolizes private life. On either side of her, paintings of plump infants personify spring and summer. Other details of the cosmic scheme of the room are spelled out by additional paintings framed in woodwork and by small sculptures posed in niches.

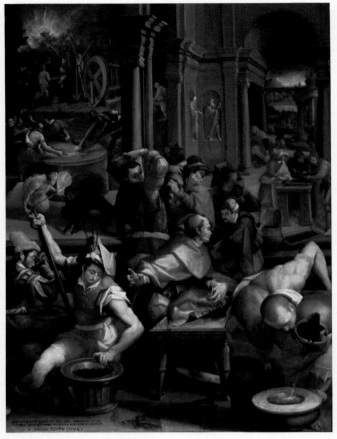

INVENTION OF GUNPOWDER

A different artist executed each of the four paintings shown on these pages in about 1570, when Francesco began to decorate his studiolo. For one of the side walls he ordered pictures of four artisans' workshops, probably the very workshops he had installed in several Medici residences. In the Invention of Gunpowder, a man in monk's dress directs the workers. Explosives fascinated Francesco, who also enjoyed tinkering with fireworks. Probably Francesco himself, in red hose and bloomers, stirs a pan in The Alchemist's Shop, a clutter of stoves, flasks, and retorts. And in The Glassmaker's Shop he appears again, standing on the left, examining a piece of glass while artisans gather around the glowing furnace in the background. In the relative comfort of The Goldsmith's Shop, where well-dressed craftsmen are seated at tables spread with projects in progress, Francesco is in the foreground holding the Medici crown. He often worked alongside his artisans and was especially skilled at goldsmithery and setting precious stones.

THE ALCHEMIST'S SHOP

THE GLASSMAKER'S SHOP

THE GOLDSMITH'S SHOP

TEXT CONTINUED FROM PAGE 141

based on the fourteenth-century version of the Tuscan language. Even dictionaries had to depend on the glories of the past.

In other respects Francesco borrowed the appearance from Lorenzo without the spirit. The early Medici had organized great pageants that involved all the people and became a form of communal rejoicing. But under the grand duke, whose sumptuous court rivaled the courts of France and England, the festivities were those of an absolute monarch, arranged to please his vanity and utterly remote from the citizens of Florence. His court pageants glorified him, and he was always hungry for compliments about them. But like his contemporaries the Farnese, he cared more about things being expensive than about their being beautiful.

As for the grand duke's family life, it soon became a kind of melodrama of sex and violence. His sister Isabella—the only surviving daughter of Cosimo and Eleanora—was unfaithful to her husband, Paolo Orsini, who was himself involved in a love affair with another man's wife. Having hired a gang of assassins to dispose of his wife's lover, Orsini personally strangled Isabella with a rope. He then married the woman he was in love with, who had meanwhile managed to have her own husband killed. Pope Sixtus V was shocked enough by these crimes to threaten to send troops to Florence, so Orsini fled.

Piero, the grand duke's youngest brother, also murdered his wife by strangulation, not so much because she had been unfaithful to him as because she had openly mourned her dead lover after his trial and execution for killing a man in a duel. Other members of the family showed a marked tendency to drop dead at odd moments, and the citizens of Florence naturally assumed that Francesco had poisoned them, especially since he was such a proficient chemist. In any case he remained unperturbed by the death rate or the willingness of his relations to hire assassins and to commit murders as they chose.

His daughter Eleonora's wedding stirred up additional gossip. The prospective groom, Vicenzo Gonzaga, was heir to the duchy of Mantua. He had a preference for young men, so when his first marriage had turned out not to be fruitful, people assumed Vicenzo

While guests look on from surrounding balconies, miniature ships fight a mock naval battle in the flooded courtyard of the Palazzo Pitti. This expensive entertainment, along with fireworks and feasts, celebrated the wedding of Ferdinand, Francesco de' Medici's brother, to a French noblewoman, in 1589.

was at fault. After that marriage was dissolved, Francesco—wanting the Gonzaga as his allies—proposed his daughter as the next candidate.

Francesco did insist, however, on one condition to the marriage—Vicenzo had to prove beforehand, in front of witnesses, that he was capable of consummating the union. Thinking this a reasonable request, Vicenzo agreed to a test. After a little research, a suitable and willing virgin was found; an appointment was made; and, in the presence of a doctor and the Florentine envoy, Vicenzo proceeded to deflower the young woman. Everything went well, at least according to the witnesses. And then the ex-virgin claimed that she was intact after all. Vicenzo repeated the test, and the woman admitted that she had lied. Francesco then made preparations for his daughter's wedding to Vicenzo.

Francesco himself married Joanna of Austria, Charles V's great-niece. That he could make such a match showed how far the Medici had progressed since Alessandro: Joanna was a legitimate Austrian archduchess. But Joanna hated Italy, despised Francesco, and resented his many mistresses. Having become the mother of a son, she died in 1578, to the great relief of her husband. People automatically assumed that he had poisoned her.

For some time Francesco had been in love with a beautiful young matron, Bianca Capello. Bianca came from an aristocratic Venetian family, but at an early age she had eloped with a poor Florentine bank clerk, Piero Capello. Her family was outraged and, according to the custom of the time, hired a professional assassin to kill the couple. Bianca, understandably terrified, refused to leave her house and spent most of her time looking out of the window. One day Francesco spotted her. He arranged to meet her and instantly fell in love. Since Bianca was married, he offered her husband a position at court. (Bianca's parents, meanwhile, called off the assassination.) In time Piero grew tired of being official cuckold to his serene highness. Francesco arranged with one of his courtiers to pick a quarrel with Piero, during which the wronged husband lost his life.

When Joanna's death set him free, the grand duke married his mistress, mindless of the scandal. Francesco spent the unprece-dented sum of 300,000 ducats on the coronation of the new grand duchess. Taxes were high, and the people resented all the expendi-ture—especially since Bianca was greedy for money and power. Francesco's brother and heir, Ferdinand, publicly accused Bianca of being a witch and of keeping Francesco literally spellbound. In fact Bianca was beautiful and needed no black arts to attract the grand duke; but people believed what they liked, particularly since it gave them a chance to express their hatred for the odious interloper.

In October 1587 Francesco and Bianca died within a day of each other, probably of malaria. Everyone took for granted that they had been poisoned by Ferdinand. He had been a cardinal and now left the Church to rule his brother's domains. He proved more adept as a ruler than Francesco had been. But by then Tuscany was no longer either a second-rate power or an artistic center. The open-minded-ness and the thirst for knowledge that had brought about the great cultural explosion of the fifteenth century were gone.

Typical of the new atmosphere were the extensive collections of crystal and glass that had belonged to Francesco. Consisting mainly of delicate, often fantastically shaped vases and glasses, many of which he had made with his own hands, this glittering, transparent assemblage may have sometimes looked almost magical. Sump-tuous, brilliant, and beautiful, these objects—the great passion of the grand duke's life—marked the end of Medici glory.

The intellectual curiosity that had characterized Lorenzo the Magnificent had transformed itself into Francesco's fascination with small, unimportant techniques. Once Florence had exported ideas along with its silk and had surpassed all Europe in brilliance. But with Francesco the city had sunk into gilded insignificance. Away in Rome, Cardinal d'Este had kept a few flickers of the old spirit of the Renaissance glowing in this inimical age. And while the reigns of Cosimo and Francesco had changed the rulers of Florence from plain citizens into hereditary grand dukes, the rulers in Lorenzo's day had been more princely, for now the city was witnessing the death of the Renaissance.

PERFECT
WHIMSIES

To his father's civic palace, the Uffizi, or "Offices," Francesco de' Medici added the richly appointed Tribuna, above, a gallery for his most treasured possessions.

By mid-sixteenth century the openhanded style of the founders of Medici greatness had vanished, and Cosimo, the first Medici grand duke, had laid claim to the privileges of an absolute prince and had set the Medici above all other Florentines. One of his luxurious hobbies—collecting vases, cups, and other vessels made of valuable stones, gold, and silver—became a vocation for his son and heir. The second grand duke, Francesco, devoted himself to the creation and delectation of the little decorative objects that graced a princely identity. Several of the choicest of these are on pages 149–169.

With the guidance of Bernardo Buontalenti, court architect and designer, Francesco recruited such specialists as goldsmiths from the Netherlands and Germany and gem carvers from Milan. They labored in his private workshops to produce perfect whimsies for their patron and to master the conceits of craft—for example how to melt and mold rock crystal. Of the many projects they undertook, Francesco especially loved to formulate mock-Chinese porcelain, to craft costume jewelry—probably worn at Medici galas—and to make gold, lapis lazuli, jasper, pearl, and other precious materials into vessels that he could give as gifts, display on a banquet sideboard, or exhibit in one of his several household galleries. Like these dazzling vases and ewers that probably never held water or wine, Francesco was beautifully accoutered and wonderfully inconsequential—the princely precursor of the Medici family's decline.

Two shells, joined and stripped to reveal the underlayer of mother-of-pearl, make up the body of an ewer, here in detail and in its entirety on page 152. The head of a horse startled by the attack of a serpent embellishes its gilded silver neck. A second serpent entwines the ewer's handle, and a third springs from its lid. Tiny rubies, turquoises, and other gems stud the metal mounts and the shell itself, which bears traces of gilt paint or leaf designs.

Ornate straps and a spout like a rearing dragon complete the gilded fittings of Francesco's pearly ewer, formed from nautilus shells. It was probably made in the Flemish city of Antwerp. At its center where the shells join is a portrait head set in a curlicued frame, in detail opposite. The figure topping the frame and wearing a featherlike headdress may be a symbol of America—a popular motif and one that took Francesco's fancy.

A gold Heracles straddles the back of the swamp-monster Hydra, carved of olive-and-mauve jasper in this detail of a vase probably made in Francesco's workshops. Heracles is about to lop off Hydra's heads with a miniature sword—doubtless once held in his raised hand but since lost. Each of the Hydra's seven heads has a red enameled tongue. The gold bracket for the monster's necks bears a fearsome mask enameled blue and green, and the gold bands around the base of the top and the tail display enamels, pearls, and other gems.

The lapis lazuli vessel at right was designed by Buontalenti—Francesco's artistic adviser—whose apt surname means "good talents." The vessel's egg shape and broad mouth resemble those of ancient Greek wine and oil jugs. Such antiquities unearthed by Italy's first archaeologists often inspired artists of the period. However, gilt accessories, such as the handle of the two stylized dolphins in detail at left meeting in an arch scintillating with many-colored enamels, were the designer's own exuberant inventions, or those of the goldsmith who crafted it.

A small hooked handle, a detail of the jug on page 157, gracefully extends the curves of its carved lapis lazuli rim. Like the vessel's other metal fittings, this fancifully formed dolphin is the work of Giacomo Bilverti, a Netherlander and perhaps the greatest of the many goldsmiths who worked in Florence. He executed a number of Buontalenti's most elegant designs, and he finished this one—to be displayed in the Tribuna—in 1581.

Four pieces of lapis, cleverly assembled and trimmed in enameled gold, form the unusual sixteen-inch-high flask above and in detail overleaf. Francesco commissioned his favorite, Buontalenti, to draw a plan of the flask then crafted by the court workshops. The mounts alone took three years to make.

As an alchemist who studied the occult, Francesco no doubt admired the deep-blue lapis lazuli streaked with other minerals—milky calcite and shining pyrite—of the ewer opposite. Ancient craftsmen compared such lapis to the starry sky and prized it for its magical powers. After Francesco's own craftsmen cut and polished the stone for the stately ewer, they finished it with an enameled swan-shaped spout braced on fishes' tails and a golden handle and base.

The shoulders and neck of the flask on page 161 sport two sphinxes for handles. Their torsos and wings emerge in carved relief from the lapis lazuli itself; their serpentine necks and classically coiffed heads are gold. From its precariously small base to these impractical handles, the flask exhibits the full-blown uselessness of many gorgeous hard stone vessels of Francesco's choosing.

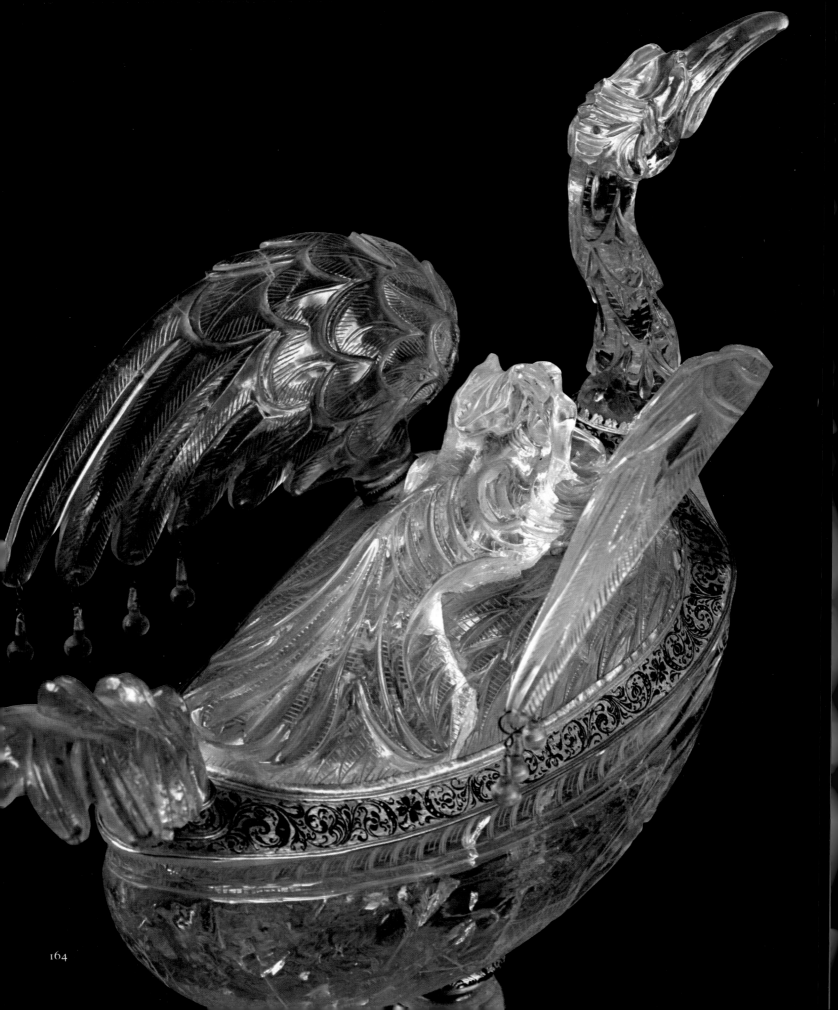

In these details of a bird-shaped cup of carved rock crystal, sinuous neck plumage and an intent gaze convey the striking force of the creature's powerful beak. Perhaps a cormorant, its wing tips are hung with small crystals like droplets of water shaken from the feathers. Gold bands enameled with blue-and-black designs hide the seams—at the base of the neck and around the body—of the several pieces of stone used to make up the cup. Artists in Francesco's Florence workshop particularly favored rock crystal for their carvings of birds and animals.

Despite its practical proportions this fluted, rock crystal vase—engraved with fronds and spirals—was intended only for decoration. Francesco acquired it from a workshop in Milan, the city renowned for brilliant rock crystal creations. The spool stem of the vase may have been turned on a lathe— a technique for working rock crystal that was probably invented by the court craftsmen of Florence.

Nearly ten inches across, this exquisite rock crystal dish, also in detail on pages 168–169, sparkles with undulating waves, ships afloat, and mermen holding tridents. The dish was made in Milan. Its gold ornaments—manikin handles and tiny baskets of fruit around its rim—were made in Florence.

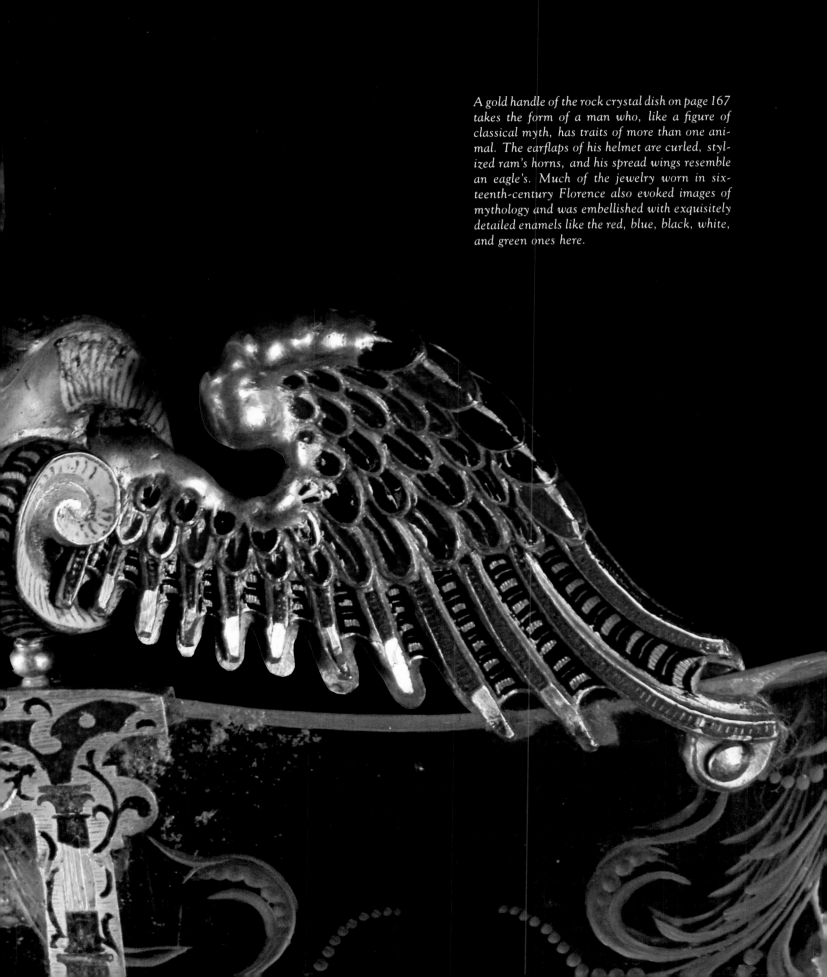

A gold handle of the rock crystal dish on page 167 takes the form of a man who, like a figure of classical myth, has traits of more than one animal. The earflaps of his helmet are curled, stylized ram's horns, and his spread wings resemble an eagle's. Much of the jewelry worn in sixteenth-century Florence also evoked images of mythology and was embellished with exquisitely detailed enamels like the red, blue, black, white, and green ones here.

THE RENAISSANCE : A CHRONOLOGY

1390

1400

1397   Medici bank founded in Florence

1410

1420

1430

1440

1439   Benozzo Gozzoli paints Epiphany scenes commissioned by the Medici

1450

c. 1450   Florence emerges as major banking city in Europe

c. 1450   Cosimo hires Michelozzo di Bartolommeo to build palace at Cafaggiolo

1460

1456   Paolo Uccello paints *Rout of San Romano*

1462   Marsilio Ficino founds the Florentine Academy

1464-1469   Piero de' Medici rules Florence

1466   Leonardo da Vinci works as Lorenzo de' Medici's protégé in Florence
Palazzo di Schifanoia completed in Ferrara

1469-1492   Lorenzo de' Medici rules Florence

c. 1470   Andrea del Verrocchio is a leading sculptor of Tuscan school

1470

1471   Francesco della Rovere becomes Pope Sixtus IV
Ercole d'Este becomes duke of Ferrara

1474   Andrea Mantegna paints Gonzaga portraits and finishes Camera Picta frescoes in Palazzo Ducale in Mantua
c. 1475   Sandro Botticelli paints *Adoration of the Magi*

1478   Giuliano de' Medici murdered in Pazzi conspiracy
1479   Lodovico Sforza becomes duke of Milan

c. 1478   Botticelli paints *Primavera*

1480

c. 1480   Botticelli paints *Birth of Venus*

1485   Mantegna paints at the palace at Ferrara

1490   Isabella d'Este marries Francesco Gonzaga

c. 1490   Aldus Manutius founds Aldine Press
Isabella d'Este prepares her studiolo at Mantua's palace

1490

1491   Beatrice d'Este, Isabella's sister, marries Lodovico Sforza
1492   Rodrigo Borgia becomes Pope Alexander VI
Piero de' Medici succeeds Lorenzo as ruler of Florence
1494   Charles VIII of France invades Italy
Medici flee Florence
1495   Francesco Gonzaga, leading anti-French league, defeats French in battle of Fornovo di Taro
1495-1498   Girolamo Savonarola is primary influence in Florence

1495   Isabella d'Este commissions Mantegna to paint commemorative work of Francesco's victory at Fornovo

c. 1500   Antico interprets antique work in sculpting pieces for Isabella d'Este and Gonzaga patrons

1500

1502   Alfonso I d'Este marries Lucrezia Borgia

Cosimo (the Elder) 1389-1464	Piero 1414-1469	Lorenzo 1449-1492	Giuliano 1453-1478	Piero 1471-1503	Isabella 1475-1539	Alfonso (I) 1486-1534	Ercole 1431-1505	Alessandro (Paul III) 1468-1549	Francesco 1466-1519
Early Medici					Este			Farnese	Gonzaga

The life-spans of the leading members of the leading families of the Renaissance are shown, in gray bars, against the principal events of the age.

EVENTS

(cont'd) (cont'd) (cont'd)

ART AND ARCHITECTURE

(cont'd)

Year	EVENTS	ART AND ARCHITECTURE
1500		
1510	1509 Francesco Gonzaga captured by Venetians	1506 Lodovico Ariosto begins *Orlando Furioso*
		1513 Niccolò Machiavelli writes *The Prince*
	r. 1515–1547 Francis I, king of France	1515 Rafael paints portrait of Baldassare Castiglione
	r. 1519–1556 Charles V, Holy Roman Emperor	Alessandro Farnese has Andrea da Sangallo begin Palazzo Farnese in Rome
	r. 1519–1559 Henry II, king of France	
1520	1520 Isabella d'Este leaves Mantua for Rome	
	1523 Giulio de' Medici becomes Pope Clement VII	
		c. 1525 Palazzo del Tè built outside Mantua
	1527 Sack of Rome	1528 Castiglione writes *The Courtier*
1530	1530 Charles V makes the ruler of Mantua a duke, no longer marchese	
	1534 Alessandro Farnese becomes Pope Paul III	1534–1541 Paul III commissions Michelangelo to paint *Last Judgment*
	1537 Cosimo the Great becomes duke of Florence	
1540	1539 Paul III makes Ippolito d'Este cardinal of Ferrara	
	1542 War breaks out between Spain and France	
	1545 Paul III gives Pier Luigi Farnese the duchies of Parma and Piacenza	
	Paul III opens Council of Trent to undertake Church reform	1546 Michelangelo takes over as designer of Palazzo Farnese
	1547 Pier Luigi murdered; Ferrante Gonzaga occupies Piacenza	1547–1549 Villa Farnese built at Caprarola
	1548 Sienese rebellion	
	1549 Ottavio Farnese recognized as duke of Parma by Paul III and Charles V	
1550	1550 Ciocchi del Monte becomes Pope Julius III	c. 1550 Ippolito begins Villa d'Este at Tivoli, with Pirro Ligorio as architect
	Ippolito d'Este becomes governor of Tivoli	Cosimo the Great begins work on abandoned foundations of Palazzo Pitti in Florence
	1555 Giovanni Pietro Caraffa becomes Pope Paul IV	c. 1555 Cosimo the Great commissions Agnolo Bronzino for family portraits
	1556 Ottavio Farnese recovers Piacenza	
	1559 Treaty of Cateau-Cambresis	1560 Cardinal Alessandro commissions silver-gilt box
1560	Cosimo the Great recognized as ruler of Tuscany	Cosimo the Great commissions Uffizi in Florence, designed by Giorgio Vasari
	c. 1565 Duke Alessandro has become Philip II of Spain's most promising general	1561–1564 Villa d'Este gardens and waterworks supplied with water by the building of aqueducts
	1566 Michele Ghislieri becomes Pope Pius V	
1570	1570 Pius V names Cosimo the Great grand duke of Tuscany	c. 1570 Francesco de' Medici begins decorating his studiolo in Palazzo Vecchio in Florence
	1574 Francesco de' Medici becomes grand duke of Tuscany	
		c. 1578 Philip II commissions damascened suit of armor for Duke Alessandro
1580		1580–1588 Bernardo Buontalenti builds the Tribuna in Uffizi to house Francesco de' Medici's finest treasures
		1581 Buontalenti begins Uffizi gallery
	1585 Felice Peretti becomes Pope Sixtus V	
	1586 Duke Alessandro succeeds to duchy of Parma	
1590	1587 Ferdinand de' Medici becomes grand duke of Tuscany	c. 1590 Harp of Laura decorated by Giulio Marescotti
1600		
1610		

Este					Farnese				Gonzaga			Late Medici				
Isabella 1475–1539	Alfonso (I) 1486–1534	Ercole 1508–1559	Ippolito 1509–1572	Alfonso (II) 1533–1597	Alessandro 1468–1549	Pier Luigi 1503–1547	Alessandro (cardinal) 1520–1589	Ottavio 1525–1586	Alessandro (duke) 1545–1592	Francesco 1466–1519	Ferrante 1507–1557	Vicenzo 1562–1612	Alessandro 1510–1537	Lorenzino 1514–1548	Cosimo I (the Great) 1519–1574	Francesco 1541–1587	Ferdinand 1549–1609

ACKNOWLEDGMENTS & CREDITS

Abbreviations:
EL—Erich Lessing
KM—Kunsthistorisches Museum, Vienna
S/EPA—Scala/Editorial Photocolor Archives, Inc.

The Editors would like to thank the following for their assistance: Dr. Christian Beaufort and Hofrat Dr. Ortwin Gamber, Collection of Arms and Armour, KM; Dr. Eliano Candidi and Concenzio Giordano, Villa d'Este, Tivoli; Andrea Casson, N.Y.; Raffaello Causa, Soprintendenza ai Beni Artistici e Storici, Naples; Bruno Cavedoni, Dr. Luigi Ficacci, and Dr. Luigi Lazzari, Soprintendenza ai Beni Artistici, Modena; Dr. Marco Chiarini, Galleria Palatina, Palazzo Pitti, Florence; Sidsel Vivarelli Colonna, Florence; Sylvia Corsini, Scala, Florence; Dr. Rudolf Distelberger and Dr. Manfred Leithe-Jasper, Collection of Arts and Crafts, KM; David Levy, Rutgers University, New Brunswick, New Jersey; Kate Lewin, Paris; Laurence Libin, Department of Musical Instruments, Metropolitan Museum of Art, N.Y.; Paolo Marenzi, Modena; Joan Moore, National Maritime Museum, Greenwich, England; Dr. Helmut Nickel, Department of Arms and Armour, Metropolitan Museum of Art, N.Y.; Gianfranco Paoluzi, N.Y.; Dr.ssa Janette Papadopoulos, Museo Archeologico Nazionale, Naples; Dr.ssa Kirsten Aschengreen Piacenti, Museo degli Argenti, Palazzo Pitti, Florence; Simon de Pury, Thyssen-Bornemisza Collection, Lugano, Switzerland; Anthony Radcliffe and Marjorie Trusted, Victoria and Albert Museum, London; M. Urwick Smith, The Wernher Collection, Luton Hoo, Luton, England; Meg Shore, N.Y.; Richard Stone, Department of Conservation, Metropolitan Museum of Art, N.Y.; Gerhard Stradner, Collection of Musical Instruments, KM.
Cover: S/EPA. 2: National Gallery of Art, Washington, D.C. 4–5: S/EPA. 6: David Lees, Florence. 11: National Gallery of Art, Washington, D.C. 12–18: S/EPA. 19: Liberto Perugi, Florence. 20–21: EL, Museo Nazionale, Naples. 22–25: S/EPA. 27–33: EL. 34 and 39: Giraudon. 35–36: National Gallery, London. 37–38: S/EPA. 40–41: Nimatallah, Uffizi, Florence. 42–45: S/EPA. 47: EL, KM. 48–49: S/EPA. 50: Michel Desjardins/Agence Top. 51: Gruppo Editoriale Fabbri. 52–57: S/EPA. 58(left): Rare Book Division, N.Y. Public Library. 58(right): S/EPA. 60–61: S/EPA. 63: EL, Galleria Estense, Modena. 64: EL, KM. 65: Giancarlo Giovetti, Archivio di Stato, Mantua. 66–67: EL, KM. 68: Giacomelli, Venice. 69(both): EL, KM. 70–71: S/EPA. 72: British Museum, London. 72–73: Fitzwilliam Museum, Cambridge. 73–75: British Museum, London. 76: Mauro Pucciarelli, Rome. 78–81: S/EPA. 82–85: EL, Capodimonte Museum, Naples. 86: Mauro Pucciarelli, Rome. 87: Bonechi Publishers, Florence. 88–89: National Maritime Museum, Greenwich, England. 90: Studio Spot, Parma. 91–103: EL, KM. 105: Gruppo Editoriale Fabbri. 106: National Gallery, London. 107: Biblioteca di Archeologia e Storia dell'Arte, Rome. 108–109: S/EPA. 110–111: EL, Galleria Estense, Modena. 112–115: EL, KM. 116–117: S/EPA. 119: M. Nahmias/Agence Top. 120–125: Nicolas Sapieha, N.Y. 137–141: S/EPA. 142–145: Nimatallah, Florence. 146–147: Mr. and Mrs. Paul Gourary, N.Y. 149: S/EPA. 150–155: EL, Museo degli Argenti, Florence. 156–159: EL, KM. 160–169: EL, Museo degli Argenti, Florence.

Map by H. Shaw Borst
Endsheet design by Cockerell Bindery/TALAS

SUGGESTED READINGS

Berti, Luciano, *Florence, The City and Its Art.* Scala Books, 1979.

Burckhardt, Jacob, *The Civilization of the Renaissance in Italy,* Vols. I and II. Harper and Row Publishers, Inc., 1958.

Hale, John, *Italian Renaissance Painting.* E. P. Dutton, 1977.

Hartt, Frederick, *History of Italian Renaissance Art.* Prentice-Hall, Inc. and Harry N. Abrams, Inc., 1974.

Hibbert, Christopher, *The House of Medici: Its Rise and Fall.* Morrow Quill Paperbacks, 1980.

Martines, Lauro, *Power and Imagination, City-States in Renaissance Italy.* Vintage Book Co., 1979.

Masson, Georgina, *Italian Villas and Palaces.* Thames & Hudson, 1959.

Mattingly, Garrett, et al., *Renaissance Profiles.* Harper and Row Publishers, Inc., 1961.

Murry, Peter, and Linda Murry, *The Art of the Renaissance.* Frederick A. Praeger Publishers, 1963.

Ralph, Philip Lee, *The Renaissance in Perspective.* St. Martin's Press, 1973.

Solari, Giovanna R., *The House of Farnese.* Doubleday & Co., Inc., 1968.

INDEX

Page numbers in **boldface type** refer to illustrations and captions.